Flowers for Otello

On the Crimes
That Came Out of Jena

SEAGULL
BOOKS
•
CELEBRATING
40 YEARS

THE GERMAN LIST

ESTHER DISCHEREIT

Flowers for Otello

On the Crimes
That Came Out of Jena

TRANSLATED BY IAIN GALBRAITH

WITH AN INTRODUCTION BY PRETI TANEJA

CALCUTTA LONDON NEW YORK

This publication has been supported by a grant from the Goethe-Institut India

Seagull Books, 2022

Originally published as *Blumen für Otello: Über die Verbrechen von Jena*
© Esther Dischereit, 2014

First published in English by Seagull Books, 2022

English translation © Iain Galbraith, 2022
Introduction © Preti Taneja, 2022
This compilation © Seagull Books, 2022

ISBN   978 0 8574 2 984 1

British Library Cataloguing-in-Publication Data
A catalogue record for this book is available from the British Library.

Typeset by Seagull Books, Calcutta, India
Printed and bound by Hyam Enterprises, Calcutta, India

Contents

Introduction | PRETI TANEJA

Flowers for Otello, Esther Dischereit's moving lament for a society riven by racism, answers the poet's most difficult vocation: to bear witness to the horror and grief caused by endemic, state-sanctioned violence against vulnerable citizens, and to make reply through art. Her subject is a series of crimes including bomb attacks and murders which terrorized Turkish communities (Germany's largest minority group) across Germany from 1998 to 2007. The perpetrators were three members of the neo-Nazi group, the National Socialist Underground, or NSU (the name alludes to the official name of Adolf Hitler's National Socialist German Workers' Party), who grew up together in Jena in East Germany just after the dissolution of the German Democratic Republic (GDR). Their victims were florists, restaurant and internet-café owners, greengrocers, Döner-kebab vendors, a tailor and a locksmith. They were shot in the face, at close range, in daylight, on average days, while going about their work. A police woman and a Greek national were also killed. The same gun, a Česká, was used. A culture of racism, silencing and denial meant that it took years for German police to properly investigate and connect the killings as far-right murders. In the meantime, they blamed foreign mafia, Turkish gangs or slandered the victims and their families as being involved in the German drugs trade. The media contributed, reporting the crimes in racist language as the 'Döner-Morde' (kebab murders) or the 'Bosporos serial murders'. As in other far-right hate crimes, important case files went 'missing' (the NSU files were ordered to be destroyed later by intelligence offices), and relatives became suspects.

Andreas Temme, a German secret-service officer handling 'informers' who is voiced in *Flowers* as 'A.T.', was present at the internet café in Kassel when the ninth victim—21-year-old Halit Yozgat—was shot. He was later briefly arrested; he confessed his identity and said his presence was no more than an unhappy coincidence. After the killing, his clothes were permeated with unidentifiable smoke traces. German newspapers later reported he held openly right-wing views, and that extracts of Adolf Hitler's *Mein Kampf* were found in his apartment. He was the only person there that day who failed to provide himself as a witness. He was eventually released without charge.

The three fascist killers and their enablers in the police, media and criminal justice system carried on—adding layers of trauma to the victims' families and the communities they lived in; allowing violence to continue unchecked until 2011, when the two known neo-Nazis and members of the so-called NSU trio (Uwe Mundlos and Uwe Böhnhardt) were found shot dead in a burnt-out campervan. It appeared to be a twin suicide pact. Hours later, their flat in the quiet suburbs of the east German town of Zwickau was blown up, an explosion detonated by their housemate and accomplice, Beate Zschäpe.

When investigators searched the remains of the van and the house, they found the gun carried by Michèle Kiesewetter, a 22-year-old police officer shot dead in Heilbronn, Baden-Württemberg, in 2007. They also discovered a bizarre and disturbing Pink Panther–inspired homemade DVD; the recording on it gloated that the NSU was responsible for the series of murders, unsolved over years, of people from Turkish-German communities. Days later, Zschäpe turned herself in to local police. As her trial began, the surviving victims and their families waited to see what justice would be done.

To become more than art for its own sake, in other words, to fulfil the ethical responsibilities to individuals and society that such creative work implicitly shoulders, it must honour victims and their families, it must recognize and give voice to our collective culpability, it must open a path for shared grief and mourning. It must also insist on public recognition and remembrance in order that those killed are not forgotten, and that the awful possibility of such an atrocity happening again should not arise. *Flowers for Otello* does this through its intricate combining of the court testimony of victim's families with a foray into the underworld to eavesdrop on the dead, with facts around Germany's fascist resurgence, all told in the poetic register of an ancient form: the lament. This allows the poet to inhabit the devastation of the world as 'we'—not 'I'. The text becomes a collective cry for recognition: all who hear it are held by it as colluding insiders and vulnerable outsiders, sharing in grief and in the demand for better. In this form, Dischereit writes with the fluidity of a pure and longstanding sorrow for racist harm; the work is also laced with contemporary rage against a society that refuses to acknowledge its own complicity.

As if to underline the role elite culture plays in sustaining social divisions, the lament was initially conceived as a libretto for opera, the cultural form which was once a commoner's delight but is now largely enjoyed by a bourgeois constituency. Dischereit's songs reverse this, echoing back through the halls of a justice system that failed for too long the victims of the 'crimes out of Jena'. She also enlists Othello, Shakespeare's tragic Moor, as titular device and in the central scene of the piece, to explore the psychosis of minority life. Her Otello is contemporary and ancient, an unquiet ghost, remembering his time as a General in Afghanistan, unable to speak about his wife. In the underworld, he meets and talks with 'Enver', imagined as a wise Turkish florist but referencing Enver Şimşek, murdered in Nuremberg in 2020, who remembers the General always bought the most expensive orchids for his wife. They begin to discuss what has brought them together in this strange other place.

Othello's final speech in Shakespeare's play, which expresses his existential confusion as he denigrates the 'malignant Turk' whom he once conquered in Cyprus, but whom he feels akin to in Venice, gave Dischereit inspiration for this core section of *Flowers*. In it, her Otello stands as the focus for the toll that racial assimilation forces on Black people and people of colour, while the deployment of Shakespeare's Othello becomes a synecdoche for a cultural imperialism that is the lifeblood of structural discrimination.

What follows is a pointed meditation on the cost of tokenism on Black bodies and bodies of colour as the two men transcend the ways in which whiteness wants them to turn on each other. Instead, they find a way to grieve together—a joint lament for the lives they both might have had centring themselves instead of being subject to racism's disgraceful power and its murderous harms.

This part of the work turns more explicitly around a few lines from Shakespeare's play which raise important issues that readers, actors, adaptors, actors, directors, critics, editors and translators must face,

If virtue no delighted beauty lack,
Your son-in-law is far more fair than black
(*Othello*, 1.3.290–1)[1]

Where these lines are more commonly interpreted as aligning racial whiteness with virtue, Tom Cheesman's digital research project, www.delightedbeauty.org, offers variations. The site invites translators worldwide to write their versions of these lines and then translate back into English. Before writing *Flowers*, Dischereit took part in the experiment:

Wenn Tugend mir glänzend schön ist und keineswegs ein Mangel, dann ist es Euer Schwiegersohn, des Haut statt dunkel mir eher leuchtend will erscheinen.

If to me virtue is brilliantly beautiful and by no means a lack, then it's your son-in-law whose skin seems to me, instead of dark, rather shining.

1 William Shakespeare, *Othello* (E. A. J. Honigmann ed.) (London: Bloomsbury, 2015), p. 154.

Wer Tugend schätzt und nicht als Schaden an der glänzend
Schönheit sieht, dem wird der Schwarze Schwiegersohn, der
Eure, als Lichtgestalt gefallen.

He who values virtue and sees [it] not as damage to brilliant beauty, will like the Black son-in-law, yours, as a
shining/guiding light/figure of light.

Wenn Tugend einer glänzend Schönheit nicht entbehrt, dann
geht es eher darum, wie sehr er Anstand hat, Eurer Tochter
Mann, denn darum wie die Schwärze seiner Haut gebrannt.

If virtue is not without a brilliant beauty, then what counts
is rather how decent he is, the husband of your daughter,
than how the Blackness of his skin was burned.

Wenn es die Tugend ist, die zu dem Glanz der Schönheit zählt,
nicht deren Mangel, dann ist es weniger die Schwarze Haut
des Schwiegersohns, um die es geht, als denn sein Anstand, der
ihn hell erhebt.

If it is virtue which counts as part of the brilliance of
beauty, not its lack, then it is less the Black skin of the son-
in-law that counts here but rather his decency which lifts
him to light/bright/pale-coloured.

Wenn es um Tugend geht und deren Glanz kein Mangel ist an
Schönem, dann ist der Schwarze Schwiegersohn, der Eure, so
reich daran als wär er weiß geworden.

If virtue is what counts and its brilliance is not lack of
beauty, then the Black son-in-law, yours, is as rich in it as
if he had become white.

Es geht nicht darum, ob er Schwarz ist, Euer Schwiegersohn,
sondern ob Tugend ihm steht zu Gebote—sofern ich der
Tugend Glanz nicht als ein Mangel an was Schönem seh—
und so gesehen wird er mir hell und heller.

What counts is not whether he is Black, your son-in-law,
but whether virtue stands at his command—insofar as I see
the brilliance of virtue not as lack of something beautiful—
and in this regard he seems ever more light/bright/pale-
coloured to me.

Wenn die Tugend nicht Mangel ist an Schönem, sondern deren
Fülle, dann ist der Schwiegersohn, der Eure, eher nicht dunkel,
sondern hell erstrahlend mehr und mehr.

If virtue is not lack of beauty, but abundance of it, then
the son-in-law, yours, is rather not dark but more and
more light/bright/pale-shining.

(English back translations by Tom Cheesman)

Here one can see Dischereit's thinking through the racist
implications of language and the possibilities translation offers.
Encountering these lines, and wondering whether the character as
written was racist, or the translators were, she dropped other work
and spent two weeks fathoming what different interpretations there
could be. 'When I was dealing with the NSU crimes, I immediately
remembered this connection with Shakespeare,' she said. Her
impulse to give the lines the benefit of the doubt is evident in the
first 'shining', but this cannot sit comfortably in a direct adaptation
or even an appropriation of Shakespeare's play to German, where
the context certainly equates whiteness with ultimate virtue.
Instead, in *Flowers*, Enver picks up the theme, asking Otello,

What's so hard to understand?
Black is your husband's skin, his heart so full
Of virtue it turns to white or gold
And shines as though not white: you are whitewashing
yourself, Sir, what's to understand?

OTELLO *replies, as if coming out of a trance—*

'Would you tell me then that you are Black of skin
and of noble grandeur, buying and selling flowers
                                    to please the world?'

ENVER: 'Yes.'

(Iain Galbraith trans.)

With this simple assertion, that he can and must think of himself as both Turk and virtuous, Dischereit gives us Enver as a whole community, resisting every indignity that a racist system might inflict, even when that is organized murder. The next speech is perhaps one of the most powerful of the fictional pieces in the text:

My dear man, but surely you know. We are
doubly sick when at us white fingers point.
Pulling at our ears, as if we were hares,
scratching at our skin as if our proper cover
were underneath.

'How truly you speak, and how wisely! I did not want to credit it,' Otello replies—his confession, too late, of his own tragic desire to be accepted, even to mistrusting his wife's love, and his own heart.

Othello/Otello is an imagined General sanctioned by whiteness to kill other minorities; he is eventually brought down by the damage that racism inflicts on his mind, and his tragedy is staged as a warning. But 'Enver' is named for the real victim, Enver Şimşek, the Turkish florist shop-owner who was the first to be murdered by the NSU. Şimşek was a businessman and father who had dreams and hopes and children; the crime of his murder was compounded by the suspicion and harassment his family was subjected to by the police. The poet's choice here cannot be to put the real person into the text: someone who has lost the ability to speak for himself. By not directly adapting Othello as the NSU 'story' but putting Shakespeare's fictional character and her own creative non-fictional passages into conversation with the real events, Dischereit maintains an important ethical distance between the actual crimes and the art she makes from them. The gap, documenting the author's refusal to privilege a purely literary exploitation of the subject matter over the deaths of the victims, allows for a deeper empathy with the real, and enables us to honour the victims' lives as well as those of their families and communities. Questioning how she could make them 'socially shining', she said,

> I didn't want to misrepresent [Enver]. I didn't know him, I wasn't there. I saw Otello as a King, shining, with dignity, I wanted this for Enver also; not to make Otello a victim, or talk about Enver in this way—instead, they talk as neighbours; they share the same dignity. I saw this as the only possibility. They suffer the same fate but I didn't want them to be pitied. 'Enver' is the only time I use the real name of a victim and he is representative of all.

While voicing 'Enver' and imagining the dead living again through him (even in some epic, unknown time) risks much, it also stands as inscription, a memorial. In fact, a recognition of victims' names is deeply important in this text; perhaps even the reason for writing it at all. As Dischereit writes in her own brief introduction to the piece, 'the voices of the murder victims press into the negotiations. They call out their names, professions and family status and refuse to lie down,' and later, 'I open up the possibility that the victim can become strong; even though we all know and grieve that the real person is dead.' She inscribes the names of the dead and imagines their words answering for their lives, so that they may not be forgotten; that their humanity be treated with respect, that the absurdity of a culture which allowed their killers to go unchecked for so long be lamented and then reckoned with in the most acute terms. She recalls that the media concentrated so much more on the perpetrators than the victims and she did not want to do this; they were also consistently labelled poor. 'First, as if that made their lives less valuable; second, it is not even correct,' she said. She wanted to change this focus. Thus, the extremely moving ending of the piece is a question and answer—

Do you really have to list all the names?
Yes, I'm going to cite all the names.

Enver offers his last orchid to Otello, his former customer. This final gesture is not a form of absolution but an acknowledgement of the complexity of minority kinship; it allows our tears, which fall for a world both men thought they could belong in, but which never cared enough for them, and which their ghosts, as written, can now transcend.

Esther Dischereit was born in Hessen in 1952, and now lives in Berlin. She remembers that she was the only Jewish child in her school, excluded often from social gatherings and acutely aware of anti-Semitism. 'The perpetrators were still alive; they were everywhere,' she says. Meanwhile, growing up, she and her sisters often attended American social clubs where the soldiers met. 'That's where we met Black people for the first time, and for us it was the only place where we could feel comfortable,' she recalls. One of her sisters, a child survivor of the Holocaust, married Harold Bradley, a Black American who later made history as an American football player for the Cleveland Browns before he became an actor, painter and founder of the famous Folkstudio in Rome—'the king of gospel in Italy'. Another sister married a Black American soldier. But racism persisted. 'After surviving the Holocaust, after the war, my grandparents emigrated to a white area of Philadelphia, a place where my sisters did not take their children. A Black person was still not accepted there, and this was in our own family. There was so much discrimination.' Dischereit says.

She studied politics and German at university in 1969, and then worked in factories as a typesetter for a decade: there was no time for literature. She took part in a student communist movement that was anti-cultural and anti-literature, which focussed on producing political tracts. In the end, she left—always the outsider, she had to write.

'There was always something in the Othello figure where I think he's gone crazy,' she says. 'I could connect to this. I was raised in a psychiatric hospital—my father was a doctor there—but unfortunately it meant I was also behind those gates. Locked away. This feeling of being bound, there was no air—I could understand this. And also this kind of being surrounded by people who wanted you dead, but wouldn't tell you so. It's in the air, but you cannot name it—in the end, you think you are the one who is totally mixed up. Because they seem harmless, so you think you are mad. In the end, you feel you're the only one who feels this, and you can't talk to anyone who will understand you—so you think you are crazy. You can't live any more. I mean no one says you smell, but it's there before you even enter the room. In this sense, I could connect to Othello.'

Dischereit attended the long days, which turned to weeks, and years, of Zschäpe's trial, especially the investigation committees set up by the German parliament. She sat with victims' families and heard their testimony. From the hundreds of case-research documents, she borrows phrases and language, facts from reports, intrusive questions asked by the police about the lives of the victims. She then asked the questions no one else was thinking of— how many children did those killed have? Who loved them? In *Flowers*, she wanted to make clear they were not just a 'bunch of numbers'—these were real people killed in arbitrary ways. She thinks of the text as a piece of performance art—of juxtapositions, including pieces of prose regarding older crimes, and statements derived from everyday people who have suffered racial profiling and racism, and reported these to the police.

As a writer, Dischereit had never been attracted to the adaptation of older 'canonical' texts, obsessed instead with finding her own contemporary voice for contemporary problems. Tired of watching Brecht and Goethe done endlessly in new versions to packed theatres, she thought such work 'safe', re-inscribing a certain mode of being 'civilized'. She wanted to hear her own voice expressing what she felt was most important in the big issues and emotions of the day. 'If I fail to have the words in the society I live in, then I fail,' she says. 'I didn't want to frame my writing or make it precious with another text. The Otello–Enver dialogue is something I've never done before—going centuries back in time and language, I really pretend to be there.'

In *Flowers*, she makes certain other remarkable ethical decisions that reflect on the artists' responsibility when dealing with violent crime: she tacks away from the more sensational and lurid aspects of the tragedy which attracted press. There is no repetition of the media's racist slurs; there is no focus on Zschäpe's mental state, her appearance (which the media highlighted for drama) or her tasteless Pink Panther video. Instead, the absurdity of an individual criminal's madness broadens to include a historical context in which ferocious danger is licensed by wilful communal blindness. The piece opens in the landscape of the near past: the Berlin wall has fallen; the GDR is no more, and yet attitudes towards authority, national purity, state systems have not changed. German chancellor Angela Merkel is quoted speaking for the nation's shame at the culture of impunity within which the NSU operate. The Ku Klux Klan (which some of the officers, redeployed from the NSU investigation, ended up joining via the German chapter of Fighters of America), appear in *Flowers* as quilting ladies S. and Frauke, referencing the wives of the police who sewed special emblems on their KKK clothes. Dischereit reveals the wives hiding in plain sight: their seemingly benign, everyday tools meant to sew comfort are instead used to stitch their murderous husbands' clothes. There is a patchwork of other harms sharing space with the killings, earlier racist crimes that went unspoken or remained unsolved are now part of a continuum to which this text bears such powerful and unique witness. Meanwhile, the lamentations that begin the piece underscore the enormity of grief by focussing on the quotidian: the child who had a tortoise, a hamster, the colour of flowers (red), the small feet of a beloved, now lost.

Blumen fur Otello / Için Çiçekler Otello was originally published in 2014, in German and Turkish (translated by Saliha Yeniyol), with the languages displayed on facing pages. The premier and a subsequent multi-city tour had already taken place in 2013, while Dischereit was Writer in Residence at the University of Wisconsin. Since then, readings and performances have taken place live in festivals, theatres and universities around the world; in Germany, where possible, with Turkish readers, so the audience can hear both languages. While Turkish-German audiences know both, Dischereit has remarked that monolingual German speakers have rarely heard Turkish in this form; they have commented to her on its beauty.

With the first publication of the full text in English, translator Iain Galbraith has found yet another vernacular for this powerful and important work. His fresh and sensitive approach gives proper voice to its hybrid register and philosophical movements as the material shifts from lament to latent outrage to factual crime report, from journalistic extracts to the dream narrative to end with the simple litany: the list of NSU and rightwing terrorist crimes since 1990, the names of the dead on record. He notes:

A fair proportion of *Flowers for Otello* consists of spoken language, and when you are translating for the stage or a dramatic text of any kind, you must concentrate on the ear in its relation to the actor's mouth. It's no good producing an impressively accurate translation if it can't be easily or naturally spoken. At the same time, one has to remember that language is spoken very differently in different situations. Register is of the essence. The head of an intelligence agency speaking to his own gives a very different impression from a woman engaged in an internal dialogue with her dead husband. There is such a rich mix of textual types here, too, involving dialogue, speeches, reports, critical discourse, biography and hard statistical data. What is more, the range of characters is especially heterogeneous.

His solution is to explore a 'more primary, more volatile and intimate encounter' with the source text, to operate 'a radical form of listening: that is, to and with voices'. This allows him to recompose the whole as if encountered for the first time, and for that experience to be captured for the reader. It's a perfect method to approach this work, and invites readers of English to bear witness by hearing, in a profound and present way, the echoes of the voices of people who lived through the crimes.

Flowers for Otello is an intense, deeply researched and felt postmodern collaborative work. Among creative responses made partly via Shakespeare to systemic racism, in its combination of testimony, myth and its unflinching documentation of the history of violence against minorities of colour, it stands alone. Galbraith's translation brings Dischereit's humanism to the fore and underlines how her command of form refuses chaos, instead revealing the chilling, patterned order of tragedy. We can join in lament;

we can attempt to do better by hearing what the text has to say about our belief systems, those in power, internalized shame, the potential for courage. We can move forward with that knowledge, which will not be forgotten.

As an admirer of Esther's writing and approach, I was privileged to share several hours with her in Berlin in 2016, and to correspond with her over the years about *Flowers*. With the support of a Leverhulme Trust Early Career Research Fellowship held at Warwick University from 2017 to 2019 for my project *Shakespeare and Human Rights*, and with Alexander Behr and a Swiss foundation, I was able to commission this important translation, and am delighted it has now found its home at Seagull Books.

Newcastle upon Tyne, UK
May 2022

Exposé

The work takes up the story with conditions in post-1989 Germany. It depicts a ruling system that refuses to go, together with its police, mayors and the characters who served in its state-security service.

What unites them is their hostility to the new rulers, their reluctance to accept civil liberties and their readiness to close ranks in the interests of a *Volksgemeinschaft*.

On the other side, the veneer of democracy peels away with the deplorable loss of police files at a roadside service station by the policemen entrusted with delivering them; in this case, the files were linked to the criminal prosecution of the clients of enforced prostitution victims.

In later cases, loss of this kind has been perfected to a T: files linked to the series of murders committed by the trio of terrorists from Jena find their way to a waste-disposal company.

Murderer B chats to A about how he acquired a caravan, money and basic equipment. The Ku Klux Klan enters the stage in the guise of quilting ladies. The male character A.T. searches a laundry for incriminating evidence: a receipt. Marie and XX bemoan the loss of a uniform while a cooking-programme episode runs in the background. A PERSON FROM THE ORGANIZA-TION tells XX that his position as an agency informant has become untenable; a change of countries and new identity are pro-posed—currently on offer: Turkey.

The florist meets his customer Otello in the underworld. The former slave, 'Moor' and warlord listens to the florist's story: the story of 'the Turk'. Are they not both Blacks in a land of whites?

Meanwhile, in the world above, conversion negotiations have begun. More than 4,000 former state and secret-service employees are to be transferred to civil occupations. The voices of the murder victims press into the negotiations. They call out their names, professions and family status; they refuse to lie down. The conversions officer has the final word.

With the exception of the prologue, the piece is conceived as a series of scenes with interlinking narratives. It is prefaced by a collection of 'Lamentations' or prayer songs. These tell the stories of those who are absent: the victims and their families. The voices of the latter accuse; their houses are full of grief. Through them, the full scale of the murderous acts that took place in Germany between 1998 and 2007 is brought home to us in an entirely different way.

Flowers for Otello

On the Crimes
That Came Out of Jena

Lamentations

I shop at this store
milk and the white bread
they call the wedding
Along with the change
there was sometimes a handful
of pistachios or I was invited
to try their olives
freshly delivered and stuffed
with almonds
no almonds will be
stuffed in these olives again
the long white loaves
are stale
the milk is sour
there is no bread
called wedding
there was the bride
who had no father
to lead her dance

the store is empty, burnt out
don't ask why
don't ask if it's war
a crusade
without children
with flags
stuck in men's belts

and their families shine
their shoes before they go
bake cakes and collect
the stamps on the letters
nobody writes
in the back room
someone sat toying
with his signet ring
in which the faces
appeared
a soldier
another soldier
a police officer
and an officer of the underworld
and a founder of the Firm
and someone else
he was an airman
yet another
ran a brothel
had a club
for heavy machines
between their legs
and another
who gave the judges
a whiff of the burning fuse
his uniform had red epaulettes

they dance around a Midsummer fire
first they turn potatoes over
they hold photos to the blaze
the paper starts to smoulder

they're shooting
don't you have a camera

I go back
to my store
prowl past closed blinds
wanting to give the dead man inside
some white bread
a glass of tea
the tea is cold and has stained the rim
of the glass the tea is cold and has stained
the rim of the glass
next morning I shall come, I say
next morning, and give you
white bread again and a glassful of hot sweet
black tea.
▰▰▰▰▰▰

The girl with the long hair
sits there with a comb
some of its teeth have broken off
I'll buy you a new one
no says the girl no
that is the comb
my father bought me when I
I watch her combing her hair
she has grown over the years
and its teeth have gone one by one
her hair shines
fine as silk he used to say
letting it slip through his fingers
she sits and combs
slips her comb into a sleeve
there's a packet of cigarettes
a lipstick, her key and
the comb in its sleeve.
Once she forgot
her key. But not the comb
with its gaps, not that.
Not even when she looked at her boyfriend
and nodded.

Early in the morning the woman
turns up the heating, slices
bread and calls them
it's late she goes
and washes or reads
and works in a store
at a pharmacy
recommends this and that
goes here and there
talks to the teacher
of her older child
and walks with bags in each hand
her keys jangling together
in her coat pocket
she unlocks the door
and turns on the light
waits for them all to come back
says this and that and that
and talks about school
one of the oranges is
she'll pick it out
she sets the table
waits for them all to come back
they've all come back
one hasn't come

■■■■■■■

I'm waiting to see if
you'll get me a football
or a Coke
or come into my room

at school
I didn't know
how to say anything
at school I never know
how to say anything

sometimes you
annoyed me so much
I wished
you were dead
now you are dead
I never thought
someone would

now I wish
you would annoy me
or buy me a football
or a Coke
and tug at my shirt
and say
that doesn't fit you
it's too big
for years now
I've been buying shirts
that are too big
buying Cokes

and a ticket for the football
sometimes I get two tickets
would you believe it
I get two tickets for the game
and sit on two seats
or stand
in the curve like you did
with me
I never know how to say something
when someone asks, have you got any brothers or sisters
what I say is
my brother tugged at my shirt
and said it was too big
I keep that shirt on
when I go to bed
my girlfriend too says
it's too big
when it's in the wash
I wait for it to dry

as time passed it got bigger still
I wear it in the daytime too
under my jacket
nobody sees it, except you
and you give it a tug and
say it's too big
and I say
come back
and you annoy me
I'll get you a Coke

the football
and the ticket
and give you my jacket too
the one with the fine pin stripes
but not my shirt
I keep that on
underneath
and then you tug it and
say it's too big
and say
it's too big

15

He brought me flowers
even before greeting his own family
I loved the fragrance of the dark red roses
they brought a freshness to my eyes and he
didn't even stay for soup
but the flowers that was

it is a hard walk
my feet still carry me though
I always take the dark red roses
and lay them down on the stones
he is sleeping, I say to the roses, he is sleeping
and tell each one of them
the story of when he was little
and washed the vegetables in the milk

and then came here
and slept and got up at dawn
and then his wife came
and soon two girls
and still he comes
and brings me the flowers, says
I'll have the soup later momma

Stay at home, I said to him
you're going far too far
but he loved these flowers
and it was only at my place he ate mantı
momma, he says, don't forget
the flowers, the dark red kind
their name and scent

Let me tell you the truth
he was a small-time crook
and a fraudster
sometimes he'd tamper with the clock
so he could charge
a bit more
and he loves the girls
you know the type, the ones that
and he also wore
that stupid shirt
with the Nike logo
stretched right across
his chest and he wasn't
much of a looker either
and I thought
he's letting himself go
and much too much meat
and Dunkin Donuts
when are you getting your hair cut
I'd ask
and he wouldn't answer
just carried on playing on his computer
on and on, as if I wasn't there
and he won't
find someone that way
to say, hey, shut up the shop

go home or take a walk
or do something else
so alone in that shop
sure there were customers
but
I'm saying he was difficult
if you know
what I mean
but now he's
is he I mean he is
why is he now

I would have gone
and said to him
let's go somewhere
it'll do you good
you'll lose weight
and a new pair of pants
good shoes
know what I mean
but now he is
is he I mean he is
why is he now

Child and Dad

Tying your kid's laces

phoning mom

picking your other kid up from school

taking them swimming

waiting and reading the paper or smoking

then buying something for sport

pants and once a week

to the religion class

I had never won

the Who's Who in the Koran competition

and you wanted to study with me

dad—or assemble the ship

with me—or

you wanted some peace and quiet

we went home

you said for you

for me the streets of Istanbul

were lovely, just lovely: İstiklal Caddesi

or Dolmabahçe Sarayı

to Halıcıoğlu, the street where the dentist

lived, I wanted to keep going—to the sea

or back to the Rheinstraße

perhaps best to the Rheinstraße

my pets were there

pets weren't for you

but I had a tortoise

a hamster

can you stop now

I'm stopping.

But this is just to tell you

that I finished school

that I'm studying

that I read a lot of books

that I have my exams tomorrow

I'll be back tomorrow

to tell you

about my grades and then bring

you

my degree thesis

and leave it here

weigh it down with stones

so it doesn't fly away

■■■■■■■■■

A Woman Speaks to her Dead Husband

I'm sitting in the crown
of a palm
high above the sea
I climb down slowly
buy you some gözleme
comb my hair
till its red sheen
and you can smell me
I can still smell you
your skin, your feet
you had small feet
for a man and the hands
of a youth
what you did with them
on our wedding day
my hands were red with henna
the guests threw money in the air
the orchestra played
and you know it still
strikes up for me and
plays every night
they won't stop playing
in the morning I am
soaked with sweat
and haven't danced since
I wish the orchestra would
lay their instruments aside
I'd bow to them
the musicians should go

I can't hear their notes
I can only see
how they play
can you see them?
We should go to bed.
Soon, you say, soon.
I close my eyes
don't want to see them
not tonight
take them with you
I beg you
you don't answer
you never answer
answer me
I'm asking you
I ask you repeatedly
and you never answer
forgive me, my love

how can I be angry with you
please—they should take
their instruments with them
and their songs
especially those magical ones
the ones by Zülfü Livaneli
you remember the one
that we
take your instruments away
just take them away

———

Scenes and Sets

INSTEAD OF A PROLOGUE

'Ladies and gentlemen, we are talking about the last century; I ask you not to forget that!' The man had raised his forearm, hand outstretched, and, for a moment, maintained this posture, underlining as it did the tenor of his words.

His audience kept their eyes on him and said little. One, who had worked in police administration, was still part of last-century conditions. The speaker had mentioned bleak prospects for reconstruction in the East and the precarious position of the police and intelligence agencies in Thuringia and other federal states in Eastern Germany.

I had a feeling I knew what he was talking about. One morning, the couple who ran the seminar venue had taken me aside. The woman had her white apron on, but her face was flushed and looked a little swollen. The caretaker had been found dead, lying in a pool of his own blood; he had evidently been on his way home. He was a short, brawny-looking man, taciturn too. It wasn't clear where he was from. Apparently, he had often changed jobs and had even been to sea: in East German terms, an unusual biography. How he had ended up at the church centre, nobody could explain. I disliked having to cross his path, especially when I was alone. I found it more unpleasant even than encountering the woman with the hunchback. There were whispers she was the spawn of incest between a high-ranking Nazi and his sister. In a home as a small child, a hot, heavy lamp had fallen on her naked body. She had been disabled ever since, but escaped 'euthanasia' owing to the high status of her guardians. She would bump into me unexpectedly, emerging from some corner or other where she had been mopping the floor or dusting off the cobwebs. Her apron was buttoned at the front from top to bottom; it had an irregular greeny-black pattern, with tiny islands left white. The couple thought it was their Christian duty to make a statement. The police had been and gone, but hadn't questioned them.

'You know,' said the woman, 'he had a wife, didn't he, and a life policy. He only took out this policy recently; and only got married recently. You know what I mean?' she asked. 'The bit about the life policy is something the police have to know, isn't it.'

'Yes,' I replied, 'you ought to tell them about that.'

'But,' said the woman, 'but—I just can't . . . d'you understand?' And she pressed her arms and hands to her ribs so that her breasts shook and lifted a little in their cups. She repeated this gesture a number of times, pressing her hands upwards then letting her arms fall back to her sides. 'If I end up getting the wrong person, then . . . ' She did not complete the sentence. She did not want to run the risk of the caretaker also belonging to the 'Firm'. She wouldn't know where to go then, with her husband, the deacon, who was now quite old. Eventually, I agreed. I'd deal with it. I . . . did a bit of reconnaissance. Asked a girlfriend who had been in jail in the former GDR; there was nothing dubious about her—soon enough, I had the telephone number of a policewoman who worked in the Youth department. 'Youth,' I said, 'that's not right, is it?' 'No, it's the wrong department,' my informant replied, 'but she'll put you through to somebody in the murder squad who she thinks is OK. It's the only way of doing it.'

The woman watched me from behind a curtain as I walked over to the phone box. The thought flashed through my mind that my kids were still young. The coins rattled quietly as they slid through the slit. I gave my name and the name of the couple and the name of the dead man and said that the couple wanted to make a statement. 'Thank you,' said the voice at the other end—not asking why I hadn't called the homicide squad myself. A couple of weeks later, I enquired how things had been. Two policemen had come by, and the couple had made their statements. The police had accessed the house from the lakeside, and had left that way too. Which meant they passed the new ferry jetty—Einstein is supposed to have liked sitting there, but that could only have been for a single summer because then he had to stay in the US because of the Nazis. An Italian restaurant had started up by the new jetty; its front door was locked up now. It had become pretty popular, and day-trippers, after pizza or pasta, would sit there over a grappa or espresso, waiting to cross on the last ferry. The place is also supposed to have sold ice-cream, homemade Italian ice-cream.

Could these policemen have been the same ones who were sent to take statements back then? Nobody was arrested or charged. Not one of the six young people who had been there that night and battered the waiter to death.

Since then the restaurant had remained closed. 'They're still just children,' someone had said, and someone else said: 'What were they supposed to be doing here anyway?' The children, like their parents, belonged to the past century, and they couldn't bear these new conditions. What they found especially hard was democracy, they said, and they would have felt quite happy to put on their FDJ-uniforms again. Their parents still had their old uniforms in the closet, after all, even their Czech-made revolvers.

The policemen have passed the jetty twice today. They didn't stop. The deputy mayor didn't stop either. Back then, he had told the two policemen they could take a look around if they wanted but he had already done so and there was nothing there. The policemen nodded and noted down: nothing there, evidently.

It was the last I heard of the caretaker. Later, when they were clearing the house out, I picked up two wooden stools and a white garden table. The stools were handmade and very stable, the struts fast and not a nail between them. Leaving my office with its creaking floorboard and warped linoleum, I carried the box back to the car. I'd certainly used far fewer of the Constitution brochures than expected. I was handing them out for free, but most people said it was not something they needed.

After a while I discovered I didn't like Italian ice-cream any more. I can't get rid of the lingering, slightly metallic taste on my tongue. I don't know whether I should tell my doctor about it. At the end of the century, afterwards, I took a very hot bath; I remember that very well.

The man was sent on his way, as was his support team: the German Bundestag's Committee of Inquiry into the murders by the NSU (National Socialist Underground) had heard quite enough for one day. After all that, I almost forgot to mention how the German Constitution, which I no longer needed at the time, was taken to Thuringia. Though I later discovered that it had never arrived. I had sent it to the Central Politics Office, but the post office must have thought the address meant the Office for the Protection of the Constitution. It's safe to say that somebody there will have relieved the postman of the package, and that since then it's been kept by the authorities, and that I won't be able to get hold of it again.

_____ A

How come your caravan's in the living-room?

B _____

Everyone keeps their caravan indoors.
You, too.

_____ A

No, we don't, we don't have a caravan.

B _____

That's a pity. We love our caravan, that's
why we've brought it inside.

_____ A

Can I go in?

B _____

No.—Or rather yes.
Why not, after all? Come on. This
is where you switch the light on, and off.
Bino installed a TV for us, and
wires so we can transfer stuff to the screen.

_____ A

You could do that at home.

B _____

This way we can just stop wherever we want.
No need to bother with some idiot hotel porter.

_____ A

I had no idea you travelled so much.

Sure, but you do too—fancy a Viking Wasa cracker?

Freshly imported.

_____ A

Thanks.

I like the ones with the chocolate coating best.

B _____

You can get mulatto coating too, ever try that?

We're passionate about camping, know what I mean?—

it's like the lonely-hearts ads. Got the same

hobby so everything's hunky-dory.

_____ A

And how do you manage? You use public sites?

B _____

Sometimes.

We just stop wherever we feel like it.

Usually.

_____ A

And where do you like it best?

B _____

Of course, we mostly travel in Germany—

Sweden, that was OK too.

_____ A

I know what you mean. I had a row with Emmy

recently. She'd bought citrus fruit, and you

certainly don't get them growing in Germany.
That's not on with me, I told her—either or. Man,
does your caravan stink of disinfectant—
it's like a hospital ward in here.

B _____

Bino needs it clean: keep it clean, he says.
He washes his hands after
someone shakes his hand.

_____ A

Ah, him too, does he go with you then?
Everyone's got their hang-ups. Me for example,
I hate taking baths. Yuk—in your own dirt-soup?—
nah, that's totally disgusting . . . What's these
photos then, but that's . . . Is that business?
Yes, them too?

B _____

The neighbours brought them over.

_____ A

Is that their kids?

B _____

Think so. You interested in kids?

_____ A

Not as such.

B _____

They've got three. Foster children.

30

_____ A

Aha. The photographer sure knew his job.

Must have touched that one up.

Tiger-stripe toenails. Looks great.

B _____

No, that's real.

_____ A

Right. You got something on today?

B _____

Nah, we're pissing off.

_____ A

So you'll need to take the caravan out.

B _____

Right, so we'll need to take the caravan out.

Or maybe we'll hire again.

Yep, I think we'll hire again.

_____ A

My son's into hoodies too.

B _____

What you trying to say?

_____ A

Oh, nothing, actually.

My neighbour keeps saying,

I've got nothing against foreigners, but they shouldn't . . .

And I say: but I have.

Could you put out some milk for the cats?

Milk isn't the best thing for cats.
I think I'll be on my way then.
Who d'you farm out the cats to, actually?

We actually talk to people. Something you're still learning, right?
This stuff is totally new by the way.
And I can let you have it for practically nothing.

Thanks, that's dead generous.
But—you know, me and Emmy . . .
she's a bit . . .

No problem.
Give her the Death Penalty for Child Molesters.
Isn't exactly my job either . . .
just helps me get by till . . . the
cash comes in again, a contract . . .

Contract?

I think we're through here.

They're human scum, said the President of the State Office for the Protection of the Constitution, fingering the goatee he was cultivating on his chin. His entire senior staff had been redeployed. He was not amused. There were papers in the vault the public had no need to know about, he said. The receipts for the scum's latest wage payments had gone too. Some of the scum had joined the Ku Klux Klan and now become the German chapter of Fighters of America. They stand for white purity. When they join up, their induction takes place under burning crosses. The policemen from Baden-Wuerttemberg had burning crosses too. 'Long live white supremacy'—their speeches set fire to the forests.

On 26 January 2012, the German Bundestag instated a Parliamentary Committee of Inquiry whose task was to get to the bottom of the most shocking series of murders the Federal Republic had experienced since 1945. Eleven years after the first of these racially motivated murders, on 11 November 2011, the Public Prosecutor General's office assumed responsibility for the investigation. In so doing, it recognized the crimes as acts that had endangered, or were currently a danger to, the security of the Federal Republic of Germany. On the same day, files concerning the same crimes went missing at the Federal and State Offices of Criminal Investigation and Offices for the Protection of the Constitution, as well as from the internal security agencies and its various bodies. In the following months, the Committee of Inquiry was informed that, in many cases, documents had been withheld or deemed unlocatable, mislaid or shredded.

The fact that secure-documents-transport between official bodies in the Federal Republic of Germany had been impossible for some time had gone unnoticed.

The last time files disappeared, it was at a roadside rest stop. That's an unusual place to find files. The police officers were supposed to transport files bearing on proceedings against Borys Bartkiv and others, file number 68Js55/03, from A to B. Nothing there for the Federal Prosecutor General. Only prostitution, enforced prostitution—which rightwing radicals also live off sometimes, as they do from drugs. This, in turn, leads to turf wars between gangs and anxiety among clients, especially those in politics. In 2004, the policemen parked their vehicle outside the highway rest stop and went for something to eat. One ordered goulash soup and schnitzel with fries, and the other ordered 'German herring' marinated in apples and onions, as well as potatoes and a side-salad. They took their trays to the checkout and paid, one adding a Coke, the other a lemon soda. Then they went over to the high tables and put their trays down. They sat with their backs to the window and watched the woman serving behind the counter. She was asking someone if his portion of sauerkraut was OK; the person said: 'Sure, thanks'. The man at the counter left his tray on a table and headed off towards the men's room. At the entrance he inserted the correct amount to get him through the turnstile and went in. It was warm, with gentle background music. Later he washed his hands, dried them, put the turnstile voucher in his wallet and returned to his table. He took his fork and began to twirl strands of sauerkraut around it.

Once the policemen had eaten their goulash soup, their herring marinated in apples and onions and the schnitzel with fries, they stood up and wiped their mouths with their napkins. Then they too headed off to the turnstile, inserted coins in the slit and pissed in a urinal that was the right height. Then they washed their hands with hot water. The water turned off automatically.

A warm current of air dried their hands, which they shook back and forth.

When they came out of the men's room, slipping into their wallets the vouchers they had received in return for the coins they had inserted, somebody had already cleared away their trays. They nodded to the woman behind the counter and said goodbye. When they got back to their vehicle, they realized it had been broken into. The trunk lock was damaged. The files they had placed in the trunk had vanished. The officers found this surprising, so they phoned the nearest police station to report the incident. The nearest police station sent two officers who took down the relevant details, examined the vehicle to ensure it was roadworthy, noted down what had been removed from inside the car. Nothing else had been taken.

———

Two years later, Halit Yozgar is murdered. A secret-service man from Kassel, who was surfing in the same internet café at the time, saw the murder victim's final hand movement. He considered himself neither witness nor offender. It was in this state of mind too— secret agent happens to be surfing in internet café—that he later entered a contract laundry. Jackets and pants are treated as work clothing. You claim expenses. When he picks up the jacket and pants, his shirts are perfect, but A.T. always complains if his jeans have been ironed. He has stipulated quite clearly: 'no crease', and again: 'not the jeans'. Today, picking up his clothes, he does not complain. Washing is at 90 degrees C, and ironing at 200 degrees.

———

                                                    A.T.

Hello, I just want to pick up my stuff.

And you must have found a receipt.

I need it.

                                    LAUNDRY EMPLOYEE _____

                            No receipt found, I'm afraid. Sorry about

                                            that. Was it important?

                    _____ A.T.

Course, or I wouldn't be asking.

                                    LAUNDRY EMPLOYEE _____

                                    What did it look like?

                    _____ A.T.

It was a receipt from a gas station.

                                    LAUNDRY EMPLOYEE _____

                            Well, why don't you just use one from a

                            different day when it was a private . . .

                    _____ A.T.

Won't do.

Has to be the original.

It's my expenses.

                                    LAUNDRY EMPLOYEE _____

                            I thought you didn't drive these days.

                    _____ A.T.

What makes you think that?

LAUNDRY EMPLOYEE _____

Didn't you say something about your wife having
a total? But it's none of my business.
Doesn't matter anyway. Or was it a company car, eh?

_____ A.T.

Company car? Only the President has or . . .

LAUNDRY EMPLOYEE _____

But what do you need the gas receipt for then,
if you weren't even driving?

_____ A.T.

I just need the receipt.

LAUNDRY EMPLOYEE _____

Don't look good—
just this lump of paper in the pants.

_____ A.T.

Surely you always search the pockets.
There could be bits of metal left and
then the washing machines . . .

LAUNDRY EMPLOYEE _____

Now you're telling me I have to look
for cartridge cases before washing?
No, we do laundry here. That's it.
Our laundry has f-all to do with the
Constitution. We've been going for seventy
years. That's seventy years of white linen.

_____ A.T.

Us too. Just give me the clump of paper.

LAUNDRY EMPLOYEE _____

That's right. You'll manage to fix that, I bet,
get it back in shape, no? With all those gadgets you've got.
I had a look round the Magdalenenstrasse in Berlin—
I was visiting with my friend—just
to see what they . . . really interesting, it
was. They had everything. But you left a plastic bag here
with a cell phone in it. Let's see if it still works.

_____ A.T.

Leave that. I want to pick up these things.

LAUNDRY EMPLOYEE _____

How come you didn't miss your cell phone?
No, no, come on, we'll give it a test run—it's so damp
here, with the steam and all. Right, I'll just listen in—
it's been such a while since you were here last.
Oops! I've gone and pressed that—what is that?
Is that memory? Or what?

_____ A.T.

I want to pay my bill.

LAUNDRY EMPLOYEE _____

Maybe I got something wrong—did someone else leave that.
Take your time. I'm taking my time too, but that's . . .
Here's a message: 'With you added that makes 30.
You're in.' Have you joined something?

_____ A.T.

Look, I'd like my things. I'm in a hurry.

LAUNDRY EMPLOYEE _____

Aha, I joined a club too.

Right—here's your precious property back.

Can't really get by without it these days;

I mean you've got know where you belong, am

I right? Now did I put your things under 'A' for 'Adolf' or . . .

_____ A.T.

Where d'you get that from?

LAUNDRY EMPLOYEE _____

Last time you were with someone,

and the guy called you 'Adolf'.

_____ A.T.

Look under 'A'.

There can't be that many 'As'?

> *The cell phone rings. A.T. takes the call.*
> *A woman's purring sultry voice announces:*
> 'In the cherries, OK?'

_____ A.T.

What's that then? Did you press handsfree

too or what? Look, I said I wanted to pay.

> *Woman's voice*: With rain—cherries and rain . . .

I get it. You're expected in the cherries, I presume.
Here's your package. Collective billing as usual, OK?
Well, at least the cell phone
didn't end up in the wash, right?

_____ S.

No time to spare, no time at all. I should
have been ready three weeks ago. I've set
it all up but I'm getting nowhere.

                              FRAUKE _____
                        Who did the designs?

_____ S.

We do them ourselves. The whole lot. But that's
nothing compared to what our leader can do.
This one's simple . . . perhaps I just don't
have the patience for it. She even stitches letters on
the back—really small ones. By hand.
She's really quick. And . . . hers look like she's
used a machine. She does a whole series at once.
The pink embroidery thread is a must.

                              FRAUKE _____
                     Is that all for the exhibition?

_____ S.

Not that, no. That's private. We can only
use it at the Medieval Spectacle.
Yeah, I know it's a bit odd. Someone did it once
and stood on the stage for an hour wearing
the whole get-up.

                              FRAUKE _____
                    Have you been doing this long?

_____ S.

It was when I realized I loved quilting
so much. Actually, I've been thinking
of giving it up. I just haven't got the time.
But I come back every year.

                                    FRAUKE _____
                        You mean for the patchwork?

_____ S.

Nope, the quilting.

                                    FRAUKE _____
                   Is that it then, that tiny bit on the hem?

_____ S.

And the back. Just a tiny bit different
in colour.

                                    FRAUKE _____
                    But these bits are hardly very special,
                                except for this symbol . . .

_____ S.

You probably just don't get it.
You see, this is a kind of, it's like
a communion dress, you know?
Or like for a Youth Consecration ceremony—I'm not exactly
an expert. In any case it's a piece of clothing that's handmade
for a certain person. A bespoke piece.
Everything's got to be just so.

Outer seam, inner seam, symbols in the right place,
openings for the eyes, all that. They have to be
hand-washed and ironed too
before they go in the closet.

FRAUKE _____

I don't remember you doing

this kind of thing

before.

_____ S.

Because I didn't. I haven't been doing it for long.
But, in fact, I don't really do anything else
right now. There's just more of it these days. There's
a demand. Of course, you can get these things from
the Yanks, but, somehow, we just wanted to do
our own thing . . .
And anyway, it really is quite a challenge.
You have to cut out the material carefully along the markings
and hem them. Special silk for the buttonhole stitch.
And make sure you don't damage the material
when you're cutting it out.

FRAUKE _____

Buttonhole—since the thirteenth century.

It says so in my Google.

_____ S.

Is that right? KKK's been around since 1865.

FRAUKE _____

What's KKK?

_____ S.

Come on, you know that. Buttonhole, eye-hole, hm—
buttonhole, eye-hole—what's that all about then, hm?
Come on, yours signed up too. Six of 'em went along
together. Practically the whole unit.
You've got to concentrate like mad . . .

▬▬▬▬▬▬

There used to be this magazine called 'MAD'. Mad, as in insane. In fact, MAD is an intelligence agency. A military agency, a military counter-intelligence agency in the Federal Republic, called the (M)ilitärischer (A)bschirm (D)ienst. I can't imagine phoning up the Military Counter-Intelligence Service and saying: 'Can you do us some countering, please? Can you protect the public, society, and me: would you mind countering Uwe Mundlos for us?' And the Military Counter-Intelligence Service, or rather the civil servant representing the agency, replies: 'Sure thing, we'll do that for you, Madam.' And the civil servant gets hold of Uwe Mundlos and says: 'Would you like to work for us—like, keep us informed about any illegal goings-on in that scene where you hang out?' And Uwe Mundlos goes: 'No thanks.' So the man from Counter-Intelligence closes the Mundlos File, or rather forwards the result to the agency in charge of countering dangers to the German Constitution. And the soldier Mundlos goes ahead and receives his army-weapons training. Later, the civil servant throws out the Mundlos File. No files kept here after a period of five years. It's like cancer treatment, breast cancer: surveillance ceases after five years.

████████████

PERSON FROM THE ORGANIZATION _____

A witness claims to have seen two uniformed

policemen beside the victims' car.

Heilbronn. Do you understand?

_____ XX

Is that on record?

PERSON FROM THE ORGANIZATION _____

Yes, it says so in the files.

_____ XX

In the files that have disappeared?

PERSON FROM THE ORGANIZATION _____

No. The file that is still here.

_____ XX

Am I supposed to believe what that file says?

PERSON FROM THE ORGANIZATION _____

The file will soon disappear.

But I assume someone will have copied it.

_____ XX

995 files and this one can't . . .

PERSON FROM THE ORGANIZATION _____

The area of the Federal Republic comprises the states of Hesse,

Saxony, Thuringia, Bavaria, Mecklenburg-West

Pomerania, Hamburg, Berlin, Baden-Württemberg,

Schleswig-Holstein and Saxony-Anhalt . . . Oh

yes, and of course Brandenburg too.

_____ XX

I'm sick.

PERSON FROM THE ORGANIZATION _____

That's one way, Or:

'I can't remember, but nor can I

exclude the possibility. If I can't remember, but

it also can't be excluded, then . . . '

we only send officers who can

say this sentence.

_____ XX

I'm sick. And: What I did was right.

PERSON FROM THE ORGANIZATION _____

We all did what was right.

Didn't even stop at, right in the middle

of the Keupstrasse—those housecalls.

The Golden Dome of Aqsa, it warms your heart.

_____ XX

It was the Bavarians who set up Saxony.

PERSON FROM THE ORGANIZATION _____

No, I mean it. Go have a look yourself.

Really worth seeing. Just not all that great as a

wall-hanging in the living room. Gets on your nerves.

_____ XX

The Hessians set up Thuringia.

PERSON FROM THE ORGANIZATION _____

What are you trying to say?

_____ XX

Not trying to say anything.

PERSON FROM THE ORGANIZATION _____

Don't you think it might be a good idea to talk
about the situation
with our Turkish colleagues, about the possibility
of you getting citizenship and
keeping your German one?
Shall we do that?

_____ XX

Do you think that's—necessary now . . . I mean, come on—
do I have to, should . . .

PERSON FROM THE ORGANIZATION _____

It will be for the good, definitely.
We'll cover the costs, pay you straight . . .
and there should be a bit of cosmetic . . .

_____ XX

But, I mean, couldn't it be, somewhere else . . .

PERSON FROM THE ORGANIZATION _____

It's a flourishing country—prospering. The Mediterranean
coast is very pretty. And not everything has been
excavated.

_____ XX

I told them I was sick. Other people do that too.

PERSON FROM THE ORGANIZATION _____

When someone is absent from work over a period of time
he gets sent to the works doctor or medical officer.
Is that what you want?
Or shall we just get straight down
to the formalities . . .

_____ XX

Weren't you ever absent or ill, didn't you say
'I cannot exclude the possibility . . . '
Guesthouse, horse, house, wife . . .
(aside) I was in love with his Mercedes.
I once dreamt
I cleaned its star with my tongue.

PERSON FROM THE ORGANIZATION _____

All I'm doing is setting out various options. Lilyhammer is
colder, a good deal colder in fact, and sparsely populated.

_____ XX

What's Lilyhammer?

PERSON FROM THE ORGANIZATION _____

The little Swedish place with the crime thrillers
the American president watches.

_____ XX

I didn't set my alarm right.

Which is why I didn't come.
Am I going to be sent to the medical officer?

PERSON FROM THE ORGANIZATION _____
The TV crew are with the medical officer now.

_____ XX
(*remains silent*)
(*aside*) They were his friends, and they'd
sometimes turn up in a BMW Luxury Class. It was
always odd. In front of that run-down
gate. With their suits and ties and all top-notch.

PERSON FROM THE ORGANIZATION _____
In Thuringia, they'd brought in this reform.
Apparently, that's what they'd wanted.
Fresh from university with first-rate degrees.
The Minister-President liked the
young guys best. One of them was waved straight
through to a top job. Now don't get me wrong,
I don't mean to be judgemental
—but now he sits at home behind closed curtains
and when someone rings, he won't even let his wife open
the door. Not very nice, that.
No way to spend your life.

_____ XX
No. I'm not from Thuringia. I'm from Saxony.
(*aside*) Number plates—the number plates.
They can be recorded, but . . .

PERSON FROM THE ORGANIZATION _____
Look, we regarded you highly, and I think
we were generous too. Even when the papers
started writing about that Saxon cesspool.

_____ XX
I took part in the film.

PERSON FROM THE ORGANIZATION _____
Ah, you mean the film for schools.
Yes, that was good. Very good, in fact.
We have always said we need to work on the schools.
Music, film, schools—it's true, education is
part of the job.

_____ XX
Could I have a copy, actually. I mean,
my family would also like to . . . There are also
one or two people from the other side in it, if I
remember rightly.

PERSON FROM THE ORGANIZATION _____
No problem. On the other hand, that won't sit well
with the restructuring I'm proposing for you.
It won't go down well—I'm sure you understand that.
We were also very accommodating when it came to
your people in Berlin.
You were kept in the loop, and . . .

_____ XX
(*remains silent*)

PERSON FROM THE ORGANIZATION _____

I told you that when we do the relocation you would
need to hand over your uniform . . .

_____ XX

(*aside*) If he carries on talking, I'm going to phone. That
asshole from the Amal militia turns up in the middle of
Heilbronn and starts talking about uniforms. That's just
going too far. Flown in from Beirut and the next day
he spouts at the camera in perfect German, says he saw
everything. 'Just come over from your recent
massacre, great, now get out on the parking
lot.' I won't let him bury me. I'm going to
phone. Sure, I've held back till now—last resort, like
taking a cyanide pill—but if he's
forcing me, I will. Got the office number . . . got the
dialling code, Dresden. Yep, state capital, direct line.
What could be wrong with that? We lifted the caravan
out of the flat together. That's how the wall
got knocked down and the house collapsed. Can't be
much of a penalty for knocking a house down.
(turns to PERSON FROM THE ORGANIZATION)
What about Horst—thought of him? Horst Mahler?

PERSON FROM THE ORGANIZATION _____

Sorry, he's inside.

_____ XX

I'm talking about the Luxury Class BMW and all that.

Yeah, I get what you were talking about. And now I must ask you
to leave. We'll let you know the date.

███████

'As the Chancellor of the Federal Republic of Germany, I promise
that we shall do all we can to investigate the murders, expose those
who are behind them as well as their accomplices and ensure all
perpetrators are brought to justice.'

███████

_____ XX

(*aside*) . . . it didn't look as if anything stood
between us. They called—twice a month,
or once . . . Now I get up every morning
at four. I wait for their call. I was
punctual, I was cautious. The night is over and
won't come back. I'm deadbeat though. When I
was with the police I had a uniform. I took
the uniform with me. That size—they wouldn't
have been able to use it. There was nobody as big, or
shall we say broad, as me. They've stopped calling.

Marie, did you put my uniform in the
chest. I can't find it.
It was me who . . . ? Marie—that's not right, it was
you . . .

(*aside*) Once she . . .

Marie, you know? That's the man
who became her officer-in-charge, he must have
borrowed the uniform—long ago, I know.

(*aside*) He said he had to take his to
the cleaners—they don't have their own laundry—
and then I bet you he brought it back.

Marie—I bet he brought it back . . .
Marie, I'm looking for my uniform. She's my
niece. I . . .

                                        MARIE _____
                              Have you been drinking?

_____ XX
No, I've been working.

                                        MARIE _____
                                          Why you?

_____ XX
Everyone from Greiz was on duty.
Your brother-in-law too, by the way.

                                        MARIE _____
                  How come him? He's with the Americans, isn't he?
                                    Do you think they . . .

_____ XX
I don't think anything. We located a car.
We manage to locate practically everything.

They were there? Or he was . . . . And your niece?

What kind of hole did she fall into . . .

_____ XX

50 files, 50 files with slashes . . . times 200 . . .

MARIE _____

The victims' files usually aren't half as full.

I've turned everything inside out.

The uniform isn't here.

_____ XX

It is here.

MARIE _____

But she was always fond

of walking, and disco.

Wasn't Tino there too, I mean,

he had that house there . . . No?

Where is your uniform?

_____ XX

Did you let someone have it?

Who did you give it to again?

MARIE _____

What do you mean 'again'?

I had ordered a new kitchen and had a lot to do.

There was nobody here.

It must have been you . . . No?

I was watching that Thomas Olivier, managed
to cut my finger. His minute-menus.

_____ XX

Thomas? What, that chef again?
What did you cook?

MARIE _____

Your sudden inheritance saved us,
more than saved us.
Without it, I couldn't have bought the kitchen . . .
That's the honest truth.
Curried pumpkin on rice and pureed peas.

_____ XX

You know I can't stand peas.

MARIE _____

I was cooking for myself.

_____ XX

You've never cut your finger while cooking before.

MARIE _____

Perhaps I pricked myself sewing,
I don't remember any more.
Didn't she say something just before about how
she came across a snake. Snakes guard treasure.
Wasn't that the doorbell? Aren't you going?

_____ XX

You're talking nonsense.

MARIE _____

And the king offers a reward for anyone
who catches the viper and kills it.

_____ XX

Oh, put a sock in it, will you.

MARIE _____

Why so edgy?

_____ XX

I'm not being edgy and I'm not expecting anyone.

MARIE _____

But what if you made a date?
Or what if it's the neighbours?

_____ XX

No.

MARIE _____

But what if it is the neighbours?

_____ XX

I'm not going.

MARIE _____

OK, I'll go, then.—They just wanted to say that
someone dropped off something for you at their place. A
parcel. They say it looks like laundry.

_____ XX

(*aside*) I'm going to phone. I'll call them tomorrow.
I know it's an office number.
But it's the only one I've got. It's not as if—I mean—
I've never phoned before . . . oh well . . .
tomorrow then . . .

MARIE _____

Do the Greiz lot even meet any more?

_____ XX

Why shouldn't they? It's not a crime
to come from Greiz, is it . . .

MARIE _____

God, are you on edge!
Greiz, Schleiz, bites, fights—alrightzz . . .

_____ XX

Take your hands off me, please.

I was driving towards the border, the Polish border. My younger daughter was with me. I was meeting these people, the woman who'd been a witness and testified. She wasn't happy. She had run a private shooting range. She loved forests. Now she was forced to live out here, alone with her husband and her testimony. She was officially decorated because she had testified. On the way back, we wanted to drop off at a restaurant. A group of young men were standing on the road outside the entrance, eight or nine of them perhaps. They had short hair, bomber jackets and boots. They watched as we parked our car with its Berlin number plates. We got out. I glanced over at the restaurant. We got back in and drove off. We got bread rolls and wurst in a supermarket. The woman hadn't recognized anyone. She gave a precise description of how the murdered man's legs had twitched; it didn't stop even though there was no other movement. She dreams of Kajrat Batesov. That night, quite a few people saw Kajrat Batesov. Many, in fact very many. Girls, too. They've kept their mouths closed. There were maybe 14 or 15, maybe more. Today they'll all be about 25 or 28 or over 30. They'll have families. Bound to. It isn't a big place. It all began in a disco. Have the investigating officers called on the people who were at the disco and spoken to them and their neighbours? Do the investigating officers think there is any point at all in calling on the neighbours?

———

I can only advise the Jews to change their ways: don't be Jews, and to the Turks—don't be Turks, dress like us, lay your stigma and your language aside. Convert to the West. The Jews converted once before—unsuccessfully. The homeless—well, I don't know about that, the ... With those Turkish surnames ... they don't do themselves any favours, do they. Once there was a Black man, real Black he was, oh, he was Black all right, in the same train compartment as me—can't say I was too happy about it. I knew he'd be checked, and I wasn't sure about my own ticket, but I was unable to find a different seat or slip out to the washroom in time ... and so I stayed and sure enough—I breathed quite a sigh of relief: he was the only one whose ticket and passport were checked. The Blacks must find a way of turning white ... That cutie downstairs—I mean the people who live in the flat below mine—that's different—she's not that Black, after all.

The man on that election poster looks like a criminal too. I put it to them: 'Is that really necessary?', I said. 'It won't do you any good, you know', with those staring eyes and all that. They tend to have a lot of stubble, those men. Always look a bit unshaven, they do.

▬▬▬▬

_____ OTELLO / ENVER
The fleet landed over there.

OTELLO _____
What's left of it.
Nature vanquished it before we could.
Violent tempests raged.

_____ ENVER

Did you go to sea too?

OTELLO _____

Certainly. Don't you recognize me, then, Mister Enver?

_____ ENVER

Of course, I recognize you, Mister Otello. Now you mention it.
You sometimes came and ordered my most
expensive flowers.

OTELLO _____

Yes, I ordered the dearest flowers.

_____ ENVER

But in Hesse we have neither sea
nor tempestuous waves.

OTELLO _____

That is true. But your Rhein-Main Airport
is the greatest trans-shipment hub for freight
and passengers in all Europe.
I went to Afghanistan, my task there
was to help the police . . .

_____ ENVER

But what of the flowers. Surely you had no need of flowers
for your mission.

OTELLO _____

Of course not. No, they were for my wife.
I wanted orchids, orchids that would last
until my return.

62

_____ ENVER
Did you return?

                                    OTELLO _____
                        Coming back was a mistake.

_____ ENVER
Why—wasn't she faithful?

                                    OTELLO _____
                Until now I have answered all your questions.

_____ ENVER
I don't understand.

                                    OTELLO _____
                You know, I find your question very painful.
                        It's as if I had asked you
                whether you concealed drugs between flowers
                                so your rivals . . .

_____ ENVER
I am sorry. I do understand that—please accept my
apology. No, then I must put the question differently.
What has brought us together here?

                                    OTELLO _____
                I ask myself the same question. I am the Moor,
                        the Black, the N, they'd say,
                                and you?
                So what's your story? You sold flowers—and that's it?
                        Am I meant to believe that?

_____ ENVER

What's so hard to understand?
Black is your husband's skin, his heart so full
of virtue it turns to white or gold
and shines as though not white: you are whitewashing
yourself, Sir: what's to understand?

OTELLO _____

Would you tell me then that you are Black of skin
and of noble grandeur, buying and selling flowers
to please the world?

_____ ENVER

Yes.

OTELLO _____

And may I ask:
what of your wife?

_____ ENVER

Of purest disposition and such beauty
she was famed in every city of the world
and later too in Frankfurt-Rödelheim.
And what of yours?

OTELLO _____

Ah, I wish I could make as pure a stand as you,
but it won't cut. I am poisoned
by the dart of hatred and of envy,
was once lieutenant, then a general.

_____ ENVER

My dear man, but surely you know: we are
doubly sick when white fingers point.
Pulling our ears, as if we were hares,
scratching our skin, as if our real covering
were underneath it.

OTELLO _____

How true your words, and how wise!
I refused to believe it. What was but lies and
malevolence, I took for truth. I was hurt,
not by this alone, but had been hurt throughout the ages—
in truth, I never had believed
such a wondrous creature could
love me, a Moor.

_____ ENVER

No more on that, I beg of you—I know it all already,
and then a man came by and told you she was
unfaithful, and, instead of her, you believed him. Was it not so?
Or some teacher comes along and tells me my boy isn't
good enough for college . . . did you, Moor,
seriously believe that she, to one like you, would be . . .
But no, my son will go to college,
I'll tell you that, my friend.

OTELLO _____

Friend, shall we say 'du' to each other?

_____ ENVER

Oh, I'm sorry, I should have been more careful:
it just slipped out.

                                        OTELLO _____
                              Well, let us be friends.

_____ ENVER

Yes, let us be so.

                                        OTELLO _____
                  Do you think you were the victim of a war crime?

_____ ENVER

Yes, that's well put: it was indeed a war crime.

                                        OTELLO _____
                  My father-in-law wanted to have me locked up,
                              accused me of seducing her . . .

_____ ENVER

But these are different fighters. They shoot with
a Česká and a camera. A dead photo! They
need that. A photo, it's a bit like—how shall
I put it—like target practice, like making the
grade. These people are combatants. They are
at war. I was not at war. You know that. I sold
you orchids, sir.

                                        OTELLO _____
                  If I know anything well, it's war.
                  These days they use drones, and the men
                  who guide the drones are sitting in their homes.

_____ ENVER

I don't know about that. You'll have to ask the police.

OTELLO _____

Why the police? Is the police embroiled
in warfare? I thought that only happened in Afghanistan.

_____ ENVER

It's the police's job to see Rhein-Main-Air-Base
isn't blown sky high by crazy Islamists.
They're not only scared of Islamists,
they're scared of Allah generally.

OTELLO _____

What do you mean by that?

_____ ENVER

I don't know if someone who reveres God,
like my eldest son Murat, can become
a policeman. I fear they may drive
Allah out of Murat.
Or drive Murat out. Or both.

OTELLO _____

But surely you weren't shot because your
son could not become a policeman?

_____ ENVER

Why do you ask? You should know better—
next you'll be asking my wife
if I really did run a brothel
or quarrelled with my brother . . . or if it's

67

because my son could not be a policeman ... Stop,
now ... Desist, I say ...

OTELLO _____

I apologize, I'm so sorry, my friend.

Please forgive me.

I beg your forgiveness.

My own heart too is raw.

_____ ENVER

I had an orchid with me the day they
shot me. I have it still.
It's the sort you chose for your wife.
Take it—the orchid is my present to you.

━━━━━━━

A policeman is walking along beside her, and another man pushing
a bicycle. I say: 'Esar, what's wrong? And where's your sister Rasie?'
Esar says, she doesn't know where Rasie is. 'And your mother?'
The police officer asks if I know where Esar's mother is. I say:
'What's happened to the child?' Esar is 12 years old. She says she
was crossing the road when the pedestrian light was green and the
cyclist knocked her over. She fell on the ground and tore her coat.
I recognized the coat. It belonged to my daughter, and when she
grew out of it, I gave it to a neighbour. It was expensive. The reason
I bought such an expensive coat was that it was green with a lovely
flower motif on the lining. The cyclist tried to get away but a
woman at the lights held him and called the police. He still wants
to get away. He tells the policeman he's in a hurry. Why does he
have to wait for Esar's mother? When her mother arrives, she

wants to press charges for negligent bodily harm. The police officer won't take it down. He says this sort of thing should be settled privately. The cyclist says he's had enough and has no time for this. I also want the policeman to take down the details. He doesn't. Esar's mother looks at me. I look at her. We say nothing. She takes her child to the doctor. Eight years later, the girls get citizenship. The mother doesn't. The mayor heaps praise on Esar because she has an apprenticeship. Esar's mother looks at me. I look at her. Her body temperature's different from mine, I thought when first I met her. We were standing on a staircase, and I liked her.

———

OTELLO _____

My dear friend, that's, I find it all so hard to grasp.
But still, tell me . . .
is there not a police officer here
we could ask . . .

_____ ENVER

There is. Over there.

OTELLO _____

Would you be kind enough to accompany me?

_____ ENVER

Come on, then.

OTELLO _____

Do you mean him, he's . . .

_____ ENVER

What's he doing?

OTELLO _____

He is weeping. Just imagine that, he's weeping.

_____ ENVER

Well, one is, it's just one of them crying.
My children, my wife have wept an ocean
of tears and still haven't finished.

OTELLO _____

Let us turn about, let's go away. He's drying his
tears—look—with the handkerchief I gave to
Desdemona—no, it's incredible. I cannot
bear to watch. Is nothing sacred to one such as him; he
has no respect for anyone, or anything,
using my gift like some mere rag of his own;
he sees embroidered first names, and family names,
and doesn't care . . . No, I can't ask, I
cannot speak to him.

_____ ENVER

Ask him if you like. He would reply:
'I'll tell you what: worked through 25 leads
then switched off the light.'
Perhaps he'd say that,
or he'd get out his rosary and pray to 18.

OTELLO _____

Isn't it just a sham, the way he . . .

_____ ENVER

He went to my loved one, the mother of my children,
and showed her a photo of a woman: 'The person you
see here is your husband's sweetheart. He fell for her
golden hair.'
My wife fainted.

OTELLO _____

... erect and huge, how it thrusts and shudders
at the sight of alabaster flesh and a frothy
wave of blond hair. We have never
asked him about his own wife, have we?
The handkerchief, the photo—the way the images
compare. Come back.
It hurts, who knows, perhaps still does.

_____ ENVER

Do we know his name?
No, that we don't know!

OTELLO _____

No, we don't.

_____ ENVER

We'd have to remember several;
a team, soccer-team sized, as it were,
or a squadron, unit, division,
a pack, or a state.
So you don't know what he's called either.

71

OTELLO _____

Only the gods know.

(OFF)

And the minister-presidents.

OTELLO _____

What are those people doing?

_____ ENVER

It looks as if the flood's carrying them along on
its wreckage.

OTELLO _____

Are they out of their minds?

Sweeping in this storm?

_____ ENVER

Yes—that's right. They're sweeping. Now they're capsizing.
I can almost see them.

OTELLO _____

They are sweeping still, brushing the water

this way and that,

but it just keeps running back.

_____ ENVER

I don't know if I know them or not.
On television, they say I definitely do know
them. That's their weapon. If I don't know them,
the people from Keupstrasse in Cologne
certainly do. Do you know Keupstrasse?

OTELLO _____

I'm sorry. All I know is Cyprus.

It was there I—excuse me—conquered

the Turks.

_____ ENVER

Oh, come on, forget that rubbish, can't you?

What now? What are we going to do?

OTELLO _____

If we offer them both a helping hand,

and it actually is them, the mere touch will

burn them. Their hatred flares and scorches!

_____ ENVER

Let's try it.

We'll hold out sticks for them.

It's their only way to reach the land.

They know they'll have to grasp them.

OTELLO _____

Right, let it be done.

'Hey—you out there! Hey!'

_____ ENVER

O my God! Look at that! The stick caught fire

the moment his eye fell on you, his gaze.

OTELLO _____

And so I threw the stick in the cooling wet,

and there they stand, and stand and sweep

and sweep, and it could be
the burning wood will sear them too.

_____ ENVER

Look!—the scoundrels are pouring petrol into the sea,
and now a raging ball of fire is almost upon them.
Thus shall they die more than once.
What will their god say to that, and what kind of god
would take them?

OTELLO _____

We shall take tea together.
Shall we take tea together?
By the way,
what's this person doing here?

_____ ENVER

Don't forget your flower.

███████████

After 365 and two days of investigation we must finally draw to a conclusion. I should like to point out straightaway that we do have dissenting opinion here. Our work together was constructive. If our opinions differed sometimes, that was only natural. Nonetheless I should like to thank all the participants for the particular form of commitment they showed. There was disagreement over one point in particular: whether or not the Public Prosecutor General should be included in this report. The report I am presenting to you today is the longer, as-yet-unedited draft which includes the Public Prosecutor General. This is problematic inasmuch as nobody doubts that we shall continue to require the offices—we are referring to a public authority, after all—of the Prosecutor General. Evaluating the intelligence agencies is naturally a different matter. Here we wish to give expression to public opinion, to the extent that we have been able to survey it. This is not how the political parties voted. We have nonetheless taken the precaution of playing through the possible consequences, taking into account in particular the need for social shock absorbers in the event of a potentially citizen-orientated conclusion. Similar reflections accompanied the winding-up of the Starfighter Consortium several decades ago. How was one to go about converting arms manufacture for civilian markets? To some extent, one might see the group of persons affected here as belonging to analogous fields of employment.

(CROWD NOISES OFF)

I can't remember. But nor can I
exclude the possibility. There was no way of handling it.
My job was to . . . and that's just what I did.
Got the job done, and it was not the responsibility of . . .
. . . no longer recall . . .

_____ CONVERSION OFFICER

Ladies and Gentlemen, We have found it necessary to convene
this assembly in order, at last, to open our conversion negotiations. You can place your trust in me. I have guided the shipyards
through this same process, and I have led our armed forces
through the difficult process of their restructuring—I therefore
ask you kindly for your cooperation, first of all in completing the
forms—it has to be said that we are talking about more than 16
Offices for the Protection of the Constitution, the Federal
Intelligence Service, Federal Prosecutor General and Military
Counter-Intelligence—that's more than 16 times 200 persons
plus 200 employees at the Prosecutor General's office and
Federal Intelligence and then Counter-Intelligence too, and I
almost forgot the Federal Office of Criminal Investigation—
shall we say, all in all, some 4,500 persons—do not interrupt me,
the trade unions are already part of this process, and as you can
imagine, I have to justify every step I take there. In them, we
have had to confront conversion's staunchest adversaries—well,
that is their job, after all, it's their social responsibility.—All the
same, may I ask you to fill in whether you have a driving license
or not . . . Which vehicle groups?—No, don't bother including

tanks, this is supposed to be a transition to more peaceful energy fields—but the section on languages, that is very important.—No? you don't speak any other languages, what? nobody here?—Oh well, just put a dash.—Schooling? You can't generalize there, you're quite right, you certainly can't. You see, in Thuringia, there were these campaigns to raise standards of qualification, and so, in percentage terms, we are more highly qualified here, I mean, we are above average.—In Hesse, their premise was a different one, they were more interested in other—shall we say 'hard skills'?—which isn't such an important category here . . . Oh please, do stay calm. We shall not forget or ignore you—on the contrary, bearing in mind your services rendered, you may rest assured that you will benefit from our enormous cushioning scheme, believe me!—It would nonetheless be to your advantage if you could allow for a certain mobility . . . What I'm trying to say is that should we be able to identify patterns of demand, particularly in other European countries, and if, in keeping with our bilateral and trilateral agreements, and especially in respect of the current economic situation, we therefore elected to provide further construction services—then yes, please do put a cross next to mobility, that is important. Your 'supervisees' are often barely mobile at all, that is, they rarely leave home territory. There's nothing can be done about that, but the situation could be very different in your own case, could it not? I can imagine something might be found, particularly in respect of the Prosecutor General's office, in the higher echelons of the European institutions—although it is generally mandatory there for a lawyer to actually speak to the person on whom he is to pass judgement. It would be unlikely to work, for example, if you were to limit your groundwork to the study of two daily newspapers . . . —You have to understand that would not be consistent with European norms—that could no longer pass through our offices—but you understand all that, don't you, and anyway, I am sure you are interested in doing something quite different. I mean—the days when you would have to resign from government because of some mere footnote, well, we are unlikely to view things quite as strictly as far as the Prosecutor General is concerned, but in dealing with such matters we have, more recently, tended to err on the side of caution, and so we should merely like to encourage you to consider mobility or relocation as an option, or perhaps you are planning a year abroad anyway, or a sabbatical. If so, we can come to an arrangement. Right now, however, looking at your provenance in structural terms, it is not entirely clear to me where my placement activities should be focused, or into what type of production I should be trying to convert your productivity . . . —It is not as if you were entirely lacking in qualifications, some of them of a surprisingly pedagogical nature even, but it is equally true that we cannot simply set you up in schools, even if some federal states do have a shortage of teachers—so the question arises whether we should attempt to establish conversion production as a separate entity here, whether an outsourced project is at all conceivable, or whether we should be trying as much as possible to place people individually—and as I have already said, it is sometimes difficult if there has been a prior conviction, or if there is a request for information concerning the previous focus of an applicant's employment—in such a case, it can be difficult to provide the relevant information, and this is something you have made quite clear throughout this process . . . But please do not think that you have anything to worry about existentially—we have an obligation towards you, and we are ready to shoulder that obligation . . . —This is the task with which I have been entrusted—and it is also, of course, not beyond the bounds of possibility that once we have got through our so-called 'holding pattern', we may be able to establish a brand new Firm.

I wish you all the best for your future success, and may I ask you once again, please, to fill in the application forms, also whether you would like to be considered for the same type of work again. It is quite likely that your access to civilian professions will be largely restricted.

▬▬▬▬▬

ACOUSTIC ONLY

Şimşek	DIFFERENT VOICE: 385 investigation files
Boulgarides	DIFFERENT VOICE: 108 investigation files
Özüdoğru	DIFFERENT VOICE: 73 investigation files
Taşköprü	DIFFERENT VOICE: 221 investigation files
Kılıç	DIFFERENT VOICE: 96 investigation files
Turgut	DIFFERENT VOICE: 177 investigation files
Yaşar	DIFFERENT VOICE: 90 investigation files
Kubaşik	DIFFERENT VOICE: 26 investigation files
Yozgat	DIFFERENT VOICE: 249 investigation files
Michèle Kiesewetter	DIFFERENT VOICE: 995 investigation files

(*short pause*)

Abdurrahim, Süleyman, Habil, Mehmet
İsmail, Theodoros, Mehmet, Halit

1 daughter—my daughter/our daughter; 1 daughter,
my daughter; 1 daughter, my daughter; 3 children,
my children/our children; 2 children, my children;
3 children, my children/our children; Papa/Mama –
my parents, Papa/Mama, my parents . . . our marriage
hadn't gone too well lately—you know anyone
whose marriage is good . . . yes—nice. My Papa's
marriage was good too.

49 years, 31 years, 38 years, 25 years, 50 years,
41 years, 39 years, 21 years, 22 years—one is missing.
I don't want anyone missing. One is missing.

Many are missing. 181 are missing.

It was Enver.

It wasn't 181. You're wrong. There were . . .

Alteration tailor, wouldn't tailor be better?
No? OK: metalworker, part-time tailor:
Nuremberg. Stacker or buyer or driver, best
just vegetable market. Vegetable market:
Hamburg. Owner of a grocery store, or
rather part-owner, the other half belonged
to his wife—let's just put: grocery store,
Munich. Dreamer, says he was dreaming—
lives rurally: a dreamer in Rostock. Diner-owner—
where's the diner-owner from? Tradesman from
Munich, a business man. Florist, in wholesales
or a tradesman, someone engaged in
business, or a trade, buying and selling perhaps,
or something else. Kiosk—you know, without that
kiosk the place would be dead, nowhere to go—
the kiosk!—sounds like lollipops and Coca Cola
or beer: let's put: kiosk, kiosk or tobacco stall.
Dortmund. Internet café, was that Dortmund too?
I hardly ever go to internet cafés.

It was Kassel.

When I'm on the road, I do go to internet cafés. Once I was at the train station in Dortmund. There was a storm going on and I was stuck there.

181 more names to come. Where are the names? Do you really have to list all the names?

Yes, I am going to cite all the names.

END

The Crimes of the NSU

▬▬▬▬▬	Edeka-Market, Chemnitz: approximately DM
18.12.1998	30,000 stolen, armed robbery
▬▬▬▬▬	'Torch bomb', Nuremberg: in a restaurant run by
23.6.1999	a Turkish man. 18-year-old Turkish man injured
▬▬▬▬▬	Post-office branch in Chemnitz: DM 5,787.59
6.10.1999	stolen, armed robbery
▬▬▬▬▬	Post-office branch in Chemnitz: DM 62,822.70
27.10.1999	stolen, armed robbery
▬▬▬▬▬	Murder of Enver Şimşek in Nuremberg
9.9.2000	
▬▬▬▬▬	Post-office branch in Chemnitz: DM 38,902
30.11.2000	stolen, armed robbery
▬▬▬▬▬	Bomb, Probsteigasse, Cologne. Iranian business
19.1.2001	premises. Woman seriously injured
▬▬▬▬▬	Murder of Abdurrahim Özüdoğru in Nuremberg
13.6.2001	
▬▬▬▬▬	Murder of Süleyman Taşköprü in Hamburg
27.6.2001	
▬▬▬▬▬	Post-office branch in Zwickau: DM 74,787.80
5.7.2001	stolen, armed robbery

■■■■■■■ Murder of Habil Kılıç in Munich

29.8.2001

■■■■■■■ Sparkasse, Zwickau: €48,571 stolen, armed robbery

25.9.2002

■■■■■■■ Sparkasse, Chemnitz: €435 stolen, armed robbery

23.9.2003

■■■■■■■ Murder of Mehmet Turgut in Rostock

25.2.2004

■■■■■■■ Sparkasse, Chemnitz: €33,175 stolen,

14.5.2004   armed robbery

■■■■■■■ Sparkasse, Chemnitz: €73,815 stolen,

18.5.2004   armed robbery

■■■■■■■ Bomb attack in Keupstraße, Cologne.

9.6.2004   22 people injured

■■■■■■■ Murder of İsmail Yaşar in Nuremberg

9.6.2005

■■■■■■■ Murder of Theodoros Boulgarides in Munich

15.6.2005

■■■■■■■ Sparkasse, Chemnitz: attempted armed robbery

22.11.2005

■■■■■■■■ Murder of Mehmet Kubaşik in Dortmund	
4.4.2006	
■■■■■■■■ Murder of Halit Yozgat in Kassel	
6.4.2006	
■■■■■■■■ Sparkasse, Zwickau: attempted bank robbery.	
5.10.2006 Employee critically injured	
■■■■■■■■ Sparkasse, Stralsund: €84,995 stolen,	
7.11.2006 armed robbery	
■■■■■■■■ Sparkasse, Stralsund: €169,970 stolen,	
18.1.2007 armed robbery	
■■■■■■■■ Murder of Michèle Kiesewetter in Heilbronn.	
25.4.2007 Her colleague, Martin A., seriously injured, survives the attack	
■■■■■■■■ Sparkasse, Arnstadt: €15,000 stolen,	
7.9.2011 armed robbery	
■■■■■■■■ Sparkasse, Eisenach: €71,915 stolen,	
4.11.2011 armed robbery	

* * *

Appendices

Appendices

SCHEDULE OF HIGHER REGIONAL COURT MUNICH

Criminal proceedings against Beate Zschäpe, André Eminger, Holger Gerlach, Ralf Wohlleben, Carsten Schultze on suspicion of forming a criminal organization, etc.

OBERLANDESGERICHT MÜNCHEN

Aktenzeichen: 6 St 3/12
Strafverfahren gegen Beate Zschäpe u.a
Verdacht der Bildung einer terroristischen Vereinigung u.a.

Verfügung:

Termin zur Hauptverhandlung wird bestimmt auf folgende Daten

jeweils um 09.30 Uhr

Mittwoch	22.01.14	
Donnerstag	23.01.14	
Dienstag	28.01.14	
Mittwoch	29.01.14	
Donnerstag	30.01.14	
Montag	03.02.14	
Dienstag	04.02.14	
Mittwoch	05.02.14	
Dienstag	11.02.14	
Mittwoch	12.02.14	
Donnerstag	13.02.14	
Dienstag	18.02.14	
Mittwoch	19.02.14	
Donnerstag	20.02.14	
Dienstag	25.02.14	
Mittwoch	26.02.14	
Donnerstag	27.02.14	
Dienstag	11.03.14	
Mittwoch	12.03.14	
Donnerstag	13.03.14	
Dienstag	18.03.14	
Mittwoch	19.03.14	
Donnerstag	20.03.14	

Dienstag	25.03.14	
Mittwoch	26.03.14	
Donnerstag	27.03.14	
Dienstag	01.04.14	
Mittwoch	02.04.14	
Donnerstag	03.04.14	
Dienstag	08.04.14	
Donnerstag	09.04.14	
Freitag	10.04.14	
Dienstag	15.04.14	
Mittwoch	16.04.14	
Montag	28.04.14	
Dienstag	29.04.14	
Dienstag	06.05.14	
Mittwoch	07.05.14	
Donnerstag	08.05.14	
Dienstag	13.05.14	
Mittwoch	14.05.14	
Donnerstag	15.05.14	
Montag	19.05.14	
Dienstag	20.05.14	
Mittwoch	21.05.14	
Montag	26.05.14	
Dienstag	27.05.14	
Mittwoch	28.05.14	
Dienstag	03.06.14	
Mittwoch	04.06.14	
Donnerstag	05.06.14	
Dienstag	24.06.14	
Mittwoch	25.06.14	
Donnerstag	26.06.14	
Dienstag	01.07.14	
Mittwoch	02.07.14	
Donnerstag	03.07.14	

Dienstag	08.07.14	
Mittwoch	09.07.14	
Donnerstag	10.07.14	
Dienstag	15.07.14	
Mittwoch	16.07.14	
Donnerstag	17.07.14	
Dienstag	22.07.14	
Mittwoch	23.07.14	
Donnerstag	24.07.14	
Dienstag	29.07.14	
Mittwoch	30.07.14	
Donnerstag	31.07.14	
Dienstag	05.08.14	
Mittwoch	06.08.14	
Donnerstag	04.09.14	
Freitag	05.09.14	
Dienstag	16.09.14	
Mittwoch	17.09.14	
Donnerstag	18.09.14	
Montag	22.09.14	
Dienstag	23.09.14	
Mittwoch	24.09.14	
Dienstag	30.09.14	
Mittwoch	01.10.14	
Donnerstag	02.10.14	
Dienstag	07.10.14	
Mittwoch	08.10.14	
Donnerstag	09.10.14	
Dienstag	14.10.14	
Mittwoch	15.10.14	
Donnerstag	16.10.14	
Dienstag	21.10.14	
Mittwoch	22.10.14	
Donnerstag	23.10.14	

4

Dienstag	04.11.14	
Mittwoch	05.11.14	
Donnerstag	06.11.14	
Dienstag	11.11.14	
Mittwoch	12.11.14	
Donnerstag	13.11.14	
Dienstag	18.11.14	
Mittwoch	19.11.14	
Donnerstag	20.11.14	
Dienstag	25.11.14	
Mittwoch	26.11.14	
Donnerstag	27.11.14	
Dienstag	02.12.14	
Mittwoch	03.12.14	
Donnerstag	04.12.14	
Dienstag	09.12.14	
Mittwoch	10.12.14	
Donnerstag	11.12.14	
Dienstag	16.12.14	
Mittwoch	17.12.14	
Donnerstag	18.12.14	

Die Sitzungen finden jeweils im Sitzungssaal A – 101 des Strafjustizzentrums in der Nymphenburger Straße 16 in München statt.

München, den 22. Juli 2013

Götzl
Vorsitzender Richter
am Oberlandesgericht

Für den Gleichlaut der Abschrift mit der Urschrift
Oberlandesgericht München, den 24.07.2013

Trinkl, Justizangestellte
Urkundsbeamtin der Geschäftsstelle

MESSAGE FROM KARL SECURI

Instructions for collection and shredding of documents

Message from Karl Securi
Dept. Obj. and Facilities

Copy: the Federal Ministry of the Interior/

To all staff

In house

It is necessary each year to eliminate a number of files. With immediate effect, we have appointed a specialist firm that has commenced work to this end. You are asked to arrange for the further conveyance of holdings at your earliest convenience in the interests of concluding work within the shortest time possible.

Staff are asked to collect selected files from their own organizations. There will be no interim storage of documents. It can be assumed that shredding will occur within hours of collection.

Pullach, . . .
Cologne, . . .
Rennsteig, 11th of November, 2011
Erfurt, . . . 2012
Wiesbaden, . . .
Berlin, . . . 2011; . . . 2012
Munich, . . .
Stuttgart, . . .
Düsseldorf, . . .
Hannover, . . .
Magdeburg, . . .

Dresden, . . . 2012 (problem with safe)

MAD (Federal Ministry of Defense), . . . until April 2012

BMI (Federal Ministry of the Interior), . . . until April 2012

Classified documents are naturally excluded from the procedures and schedules listed above.

LIST OF VARIOUS REFERENCE NUMBERS OF FILES
HELD BY THE 2ND COMMITTEE OF INQUIRY
OF THE GERMAN BUNDESTAG

MAT_A_GBA_1/4-2	MAT_A_GBA_1/4-0
MAT_A_GBA_1/4-1	MAT_A_GBA_1/3-9
MAT_A_GBA_1/4-0	MAT_A_BKA_1/9
MAT_A_GBA_1/3-9	MAT_A_TH_5/1-11
MAT_A_GBA_1/3-8	MAT_A_HH_3/2
MAT_A_GBA_1/3-7	MAT_A_NI_2
MAT_A_GBA_1/3-6	MAT_A_HE_6/2
MAT_A_GBA_1/3-5	MAT A HE 6/1
MAT_A_GBA_1/4-2	MAT A HE 5/9
MAT_A_GBA_1/4-1	MAT A HE 5/8
MAT_A_GBA_1/4-0	MAT A HE 5/7
MAT_A_GBA_1/3-9	MAT_A_BKA_1/9
MAT_A_GBA_1/3-8	MAT_A_TH_5/1-11
MAT_A_GBA_1/3-7	MAT_A_HH_3/2
MAT_A_GBA_1/3-6	MAT_A_NI_2
MAT_A_GBA_1/3-5	MAT_A_HE_6/2
MAT_A_GBA_1/4-2	MAT A HE 6/1
MAT_A_GBA_1/4-1	MAT A HE 5/9
MAT_A_GBA_1/4-0	MAT A HE 5/8
MAT_A_GBA_1/3-9	MAT A HE 5/7
MAT_A_GBA_1/3-8	MAT_A_BKA_1/9
MAT_A_GBA_1/3-7	MAT_A_TH_5/1-11
MAT_A_GBA_1/3-6	MAT_A_HH_3/2
MAT_A_GBA_1/3-5	MAT_A_NI_2
MAT_A_GBA_1/4-2	MAT_A_HE_6/2
MAT_A_GBA_1/4-1	MAT A HE 6/1
MAT_A_GBA_1/4-0	MAT A HE 5/9
MAT_A_GBA_1/3-9	MAT A HE 5/8
MAT_A_GBA_1/3-8	MAT A HE 5/7
MAT_A_GBA_1/3-7	MAT_A_BKA_1/9
MAT_A_GBA_1/3-6	MAT_A_TH_5/1-11
MAT_A_GBA_1/4-2	MAT_A_HH_3/2
MAT_A_GBA_1/4-1	MAT_A_NI_2
MAT_A_GBA_1/4-0	MAT_A_HE_6/2
MAT_A_GBA_1/3-7	MAT A HE 6/1
MAT_A_GBA_1/3-6	MAT A HE 5/9
MAT_A_GBA_1/3-5	MAT A HE 5/8
MAT_A_GBA_1/4-2	MAT A HE 5/7
MAT_A_GBA_1/4-1	

No, no, let's have no paperless office or paperless committee. It's disastrous that the paperwork is not here. If the numerical sequence is wrong, what has happened to the file? I mean, far be it from me to comment, but it really is a disaster. I count and count. First, I counted to a hundred, then to two hundred, now I'm at three hundred . . . It would be good if I could just keep counting. Do you understand? Democracy depends on it. Exactly: on whether I can keep counting or not. When numbers disappear, I have no choice but to ask myself whether democracy is disappearing too. One day you will understand what I mean.

———————

TEXTS OF BANNERS, POSTERS AND SIGNBOARD
AT A DEMONSTRATION ON 4.11.2012 IN BERLIN

BANNERS AND POSTERS

Who will protect us against the Protectors of the Constitution?

How many are paid by the Protectors of the Constitution?

On 4.11.2011 Beate Zschäpe phoned the Ministry of the Interior in
Saxony.
Who did she speak to? What about?

Where did they get the explosives?

Racism kills

We do not need any more clothes at the present time.
Thank you very much.

Bread/grapes—
the wind had blown yellowish leaves into small heaps on the white plastic
sheets of tents.

173 more lives lost
██████████

SIGNBOARDS

da da dada NSU
when Nazis kill
the State sees too

Shut all Nazi stores!

We murder Turks
then say they're the enemy—
a paradox so perfect

The Nazis murder
the State deports—
both are the same
racist scum

I'm ashamed of Germany.
Nazis murdering, various politicians
stoking conflict. They stir up hatred
with pronouncements and laws
and play into Nazi hands
Pigs Jews Heil Hitler Kill all Muslims

'1 million children of Turkish origin born
in Germany. 3 million Turks live here. We like
living here, but we don't feel safe,
frightened we'll be the next victims.
Trust in politics
is down to zero.'

Racism is DUMB. We were so
mad about it we made this poster

It wasn't flops or fumbles, but the fascistoid
and undemocratic mindsets of those in charge
paved the way for these crimes

———

LIST OF FATALITIES AS A RESULT OF RIGHTWING VIOLENCE IN THE FEDERAL REPUBLIC OF GERMANY SINCE 1990

1990
1. Andrzej Fratczak
2. Amadeu Antonio Kiowa, 28 years old
   (OFFICIALLY RECOGNIZED)
3. Klaus-Dieter Reichert, 24 years old
4. Nihat Yusufoğlu, 17 years old
5. Unnamed homeless man, 31 years old
6. Alexander Selchow, 21 years old

1991
7. Jorge João Gomondai, 28 years old
   (OFFICIALLY RECOGNIZED)
8. Matthias Knabe, 23 years old
9. Helmut Leja, 39 years old, homeless
10. Agostinho Comboio, 34 years old
    (OFFICIALLY RECOGNIZED)
11. Samuel Kofi Yeboah, 27 years old
    (OFFICIALLY RECOGNIZED)
12. Gerd Himmstädt, 30 years old
13. Timo Kählke, 29 years old
    (OFFICIALLY RECOGNIZED)

1992
14.-16. Unnamed family of three from Sri Lanka
17. Dragomir Christinel, 18 years old, asylum seeker
    (OFFICIALLY RECOGNIZED)
18. Gustav Schneeclaus, 52 years old, seaman
    (OFFICIALLY RECOGNIZED)
19. Ingo Finnern, 31 years old, homeless
    (OFFICIALLY RECOGNIZED)

20. Erich Bosse

21. Nguyen van Tu, 24 years old
   (OFFICIALLY RECOGNIZED)

22. Thorsten Lamprecht, 23 years old
   (OFFICIALLY RECOGNIZED)

23. Emil Wendtland, 50 years old, homeless

24. Sadri Berisha, 56 years old
   (OFFICIALLY RECOGNIZED)

25. Dieter Klaus Klein, 49 years old, homeless

26. Ireneusz Szyderski, 24 years old, harvest worker

27. Frank Bönisch, 35 years old, homeless

28. Günter Schwannecke, 58 years old, homeless

29. Waltraud Scheffler, temporary waitress
   (OFFICIALLY RECOGNIZED)

30. Rolf Schulze, 52 years old, homeless
   (OFFICIALLY RECOGNIZED)

31. Karl-Hans Rohn, 53 years old, butcher
   (OFFICIALLY RECOGNIZED)

32. Silvio Meier, 27 years old, printer
   (OFFICIALLY RECOGNIZED)

33. Bahide Arslan, 51 years old
   (OFFICIALLY RECOGNIZED)

34. Ayse Yilmaz, 14 years old
   (OFFICIALLY RECOGNIZED)

35. Yeliz Arslan, 10 years old
   (OFFICIALLY RECOGNIZED)

36. Hans-Jochen Lommatsch, 51 years old, machine operator

37. Şahin Çalışır, 20 years old

1993

38. Karl Sidon, 45 years old, park warden
   (OFFICIALLY RECOGNIZED)

39. Mike Zerna, 22 years old
   (OFFICIALLY RECOGNIZED)

40. Mustafa Demiral, 56 years old
    (OFFICIALLY RECOGNIZED)
41. Hans-Peter Zarse, 18 years old
42. Matthias Lüders, 23 years old, draftee
43. Belaid Baylal, 42 years old, asylum seeker
44. Jeff Dominiak, 25 years old
45. Gürsün Inçe, 27 years old
    (OFFICIALLY RECOGNIZED)
46. Hatice Genç, 18 years old
    (OFFICIALLY RECOGNIZED)
47. Hülya Genç, 9 years old
    (OFFICIALLY recognized)
48. Saime Genç, 4 years old
    (OFFICIALLY RECOGNIZED)
49. Gülüstan Öztürk, 12 years old
    (OFFICIALLY RECOGNIZED)
50. Horst Hennersdorf, 37 years old, homeless
51. Unnamed homeless man, 33 years old
    (OFFICIALLY RECOGNIZED)
52. Hans-Georg Jakobson, 35 years old
53. Kolong Jamba alias Bakary Singateh, 19 years old, asylum seeker

1994

54. Eberhart Tennstedt, 43 years old
55. Klaus R., 43 years old
56. Beate Fischer, 32 years old, prostitute
57. Jan W., 45 years old, building worker
58. Gunter Marx, 42 years old

1995

59. Horst Pulter, 65 years old, homeless
60. Peter T., 24 years old, Bundeswehr soldier
    (OFFICIALLY RECOGNIZED)

61. Klaus-Peter Beer, 48 years old
62. Dagmar Kohlmann, 26 years old

1996

63. Patricia Wright, 23 years old
   (OFFICIALLY RECOGNIZED)
64. Sven Beuter, 23 years old
   (OFFICIALLY RECOGNIZED)
65. Martin Kemming, 26 years old
   (OFFICIALLY RECOGNIZED)
66. Bernd G., 43 years old, businessman
67. Boris Morawek, 26 years old
68. Werner Weickum, 44 years old, electrician
69. Andreas Götz, 34 years old
70. Achmed Bachir, 30 years old, asylum seeker
   (OFFICIALLY RECOGNIZED)

1997

71. Phan Van Toau, 42 years old
72. Frank Böttcher, 17 years old
   (OFFICIALLY RECOGNIZED)
73. Antonio Melis, 37 years old
74. Stefan Grage, police officer
   (OFFICIALLY RECOGNIZED)
75. Olaf Schmidke
76. Chris Danneil
77. Horst Gens, 50 years old, unemployed
78. Augustin Blotzki, 59 years old, unemployed
   (OFFICIALLY RECOGNIZED)
79. Matthias S., 39 years old
80. Georg V., 46 years old
81. Josef Anton Gera, 59 years old, pensioner

1998

82. Jana Georgi, 14 years old
83. Nuno Lourenco, joiner
   (OFFICIALLY RECOGNIZED)

1999

84. Farid Guendoul alias Omar Ben Noui, 28 years old, asylum seeker
   (OFFICIALLY RECOGNIZED)
85. Egon Efferts, 58 years old, early retired
86. Peter Deutschmann, 44 years old, welfare recipient
   (OFFICIALLY RECOGNIZED)
87. Carlos Fernando, 35 years old
   (OFFICIALLY RECOGNIZED)
88. Patrick Thürmer, 17 years old, apprentice
   (OFFICIALLY RECOGNIZED)
89. Kurt Schneider, 38 years old, welfare recipient
90. Hans-Werner Gärtner, 37 years old
91. Daniela Peyerl, 18 years old
92. Karl-Heinz Lietz, 54 years old
93. Horst Zillenbiller, 60 years old
94. Ruth Zillenbiller, 59 years old
95. Jörg Danek, 39 years old

2000

96. Bernd Schmidt, 52 years old, homeless glass designer
97. Helmut Sackers, 60 years old
98. Dieter Eich, welfare recipient
99. Falko Lüdtke, 22 years old
100. Alberto Adriano, 39 years old
   (OFFICIALLY RECOGNIZED)
101. Thomas Goretzky, 35 years old, police officer
102. Yvonne Hachtkemper, 34 years old, police officer
103. Matthias Larisch von Woitowitz, 35 years old, police officer

104. Klaus-Dieter Gerecke, homeless
105. Jürgen Seifert, 52 years old, homeless
106. Norbert Plath, 51 years old, homeless
(OFFICIALLY RECOGNIZED)
107. Enver Şimşek, 38 years old
(OFFICIALLY RECOGNIZED)
108. Malte Lerch, 45 years old, homeless
(OFFICIALLY RECOGNIZED)
109. Eckhardt Rütz, 42 years old, homeless
(OFFICIALLY RECOGNIZED)

2001

110. Willi Worg, 38 years old
111. Mohammed Belhadj, 31 years old, asylum seeker
112. Abdurrahim Özüdoğru, 49 years old
(OFFICIALLY RECOGNIZED)
113. Süleyman Taşköprü, 31 years old
(OFFICIALLY RECOGNIZED)
114. Klaus-Dieter Harms, 61 years old
115. Dieter Manzke, 61 years old, homeless
(OFFICIALLY RECOGNIZED)
116. Dorit Botts, 54 years old, shopkeeper
117. Habil Kılıç, 38 years old
(OFFICIALLY RECOGNIZED)

2002

118. Kajrat Batesov, 24 years old
119. Ronald Masch, 29 years old, roofer
120. Marinus Schöberl, 17 years old
(OFFICIALLY RECOGNIZED)
121. Ahmet Sarlak, 19 years old, apprentice

2003

122. Hartmut Balzke, 48 years old
123. Andreas Oertel, 40 years old
124. Enrico Schreiber, 25 years old
125. Gerhard Fischhöder, 49 years old
126. Hartmut Nickel, 61 years old
127. Mechthild Bucksteeg, 53 years old
128. Alja Nickel, 26 years old
129. Viktor Filimonov, 15 years old
130. Aleksander Schleicher, 17 years old
131. Waldemar Ickert, 16 years old

2004

132. Oleg Valgar, 27 years old
133. Martin Görges, 46 years old
134. Mehmet Turgut, 25 years old
    (OFFICIALLY RECOGNIZED)

2005

135. Thomas Schulz, 32 years old
136. İsmail Yaşar, 50 years old
    (OFFICIALLY RECOGNIZED)
137. Theodoros Boulgarides, 41 years old
    (OFFICIALLY RECOGNIZED)
138. Tim Maier, 20 years old

2006

139. Andreas Pietrzak, 41 years old
140. Mehmet Kubaşik, 39 years old
    (OFFICIALLY RECOGNIZED)
141. Halit Yozgat, 21 years old
    (OFFICIALLY RECOGNIZED)

2007

142. Michèle Kiesewetter, 22 years old
   (OFFICIALLY RECOGNIZED)
143. M.S., 17 years old

2008

144. Peter Siebert, 40 years old
145. Bernd Köhler, 55 years old
   (OFFICIALLY RECOGNIZED)
146. Karl-Heinz Teichmann, 59 years old
147. Hans-Joachim Sbrzesny, 50 years old
148. Rick Langenstein, 20 years old
   (OFFICIALLY RECOGNIZED)

2009

149. Marwa El-Sherbiny, 31 years old
   (OFFICIALLY RECOGNIZED)

2010

150. Kamal Kilade, 19 years old
   (OFFICIALLY RECOGNIZED)

2011

151. André K., 50 years old

2012

152. Klaus-Peter Kühn, 59 years old

━━━━━━

An annotated version of this list, including details relating to individual victims, was published by Heike Kleffner, Johannes Radke, Toralf Staud and Frank Jansen in Tagesspiegel and on ZEIT-online (bityl.co/CACc). The list does not claim to be comprehensive. It must be supposed that the number of unreported and undetected cases, especially murders of homeless persons, is very high. The German government, which has recognized 63 to be the total number of fatal victims of rightwing violence in the named time span, has recently expressed doubts in the correctness of this figure. The Federal Office of Criminal Investigation has been charged with conducting a new inquiry. They are to re-examine 746 suspicious cases with a total of 849 victims in the period between 1990 and 2011.

Everywhere you look it says 63. Why 63?—the government speaks of 63 dead—while those not 'officially recognized' do not exist: dead who do not exist, murdered people who do not exist—those who do not exist are forgotten—more have not been recognized than have— the souls of the murdered have no place to go. Sometimes they come and sit next to me or above me—at other times, they aren't there at all. Mostly, they are not there. 181 people, and the list does not claim to be comprehensive, does not claim to be comprehensive— . . .

█████████

For a program on Deutschlandradio Kultur to coincide with the start of the NSU trial, Esther Dischereit contributed a series of portraits of individuals who wanted to know how such events could have happened. The portraits were broadcast daily at 11.55 a.m. between 15 and 19 April 2013. Slightly revised versions are reprinted here with kind permission of Deutschlandradio Kultur.

(1) Mario Melzer, police officer, Erfurt
DUBIOUS PRACTICES DURING NSU-INVESTIGATIONS

Police officer Mario Melzer criticized the failings of the search operation against the neo-Nazi trio as early as 1998.

Mario Melzer does not work for the Office for the Protection of the Constitution. There could be no place there for someone like him. Even the name makes light of its true nature, says Melzer. Mario Melzer is a policeman and a Christian.

'My beliefs oblige me to weigh up every action I take, including actions of a professional nature, with my own morality. As a civil servant, I am free to remonstrate. We are all obliged to consider whether a directive is correct or not, and my own Christian commitment and ethics have helped me develop a professional ethics I can stand by.'

Mario Melzer has his doubts about whether it was really the authorities' intention to arrest the terrorist threesome. In 1998, unexplained circumstances enabled Böhnhardt, Mundlos and Zschäpe to escape arrest in Jena. Is it possible that somebody wanted them out of sight? Why was it that the State Prosecutor happened to be ill, the officer leading the investigation was on a training course and that the police were given insufficient technical support?

At the time in question, Mario Melzer himself was delegated to a different location, although he had more experience in rightwing extremism than any of his colleagues. Did someone see him as a risk, as someone whose investigative zeal needed to be held in check?

'I am 43 years old. I was born in 1970 in Erfurt, where I was brought up a Christian in an ecumenical household. My father was arrested and imprisoned in the 1950s for attempting to leave the GDR.'

One of his brothers was expelled from university and the other was a military-service objector.

'I was the Third Man, so to speak. Well, the GDR was not really my kind of place either.'

He was supposed to have a career as a gardener, a profession he came to love. But his firm went bankrupt after 1989. The police were looking for new people and Mario Melzer was interested in joining an environmental crime department. He joined the police and was assigned to various investigative units.

When Melzer questioned Beate Zschäpe at the end of the 90s, he was part of 'Soko Rex', a special commission investigating cases of rightwing extremism. 'They were playing cat and mouse with us,' according to Melzer. How come that whenever a search warrant was issued, they knew in advance what material to remove?

Two years later, Soko Rex was dissolved and a different commission set up: the investigation team EG Tex, later EG Zex, with constantly changing personnel. Melzer had already led investigations into bomb hoaxes in Jena's market square, and into a puppet figure intended to vilify Ignatz Bubis, the then President of the Central Council of Jews in Germany, who was shortly to arrive in Jena. Now, however, he was no longer involved in the investigations.

Again and again, tracks were covered and clues concealed. One day, the officer in charge of Investigation Team Zex, a police colleague of Melzer's called Achim Koch, was found dead. An apparent suicide. His suicide note has been kept under lock and key ever since. Even the Bundestag's Committee of Inquiry was unable to get a look at it. Following Melzer's inspection of files originally submitted by himself, he was able to ascertain that they had been altered.

'I phoned a Benedictine monk, a friend called Aurelian, and asked if I could enter his monastery in St Ottilien for a while to prepare myself.'

That was before Melzer appeared before the German Bundestag's Committee of Inquiry. As Police Inspector at the State of Thuringia's Office of Criminal Investigation, he delivered a two-hour long personal statement in January this year, in which he exposed dubious practices by colleagues, judges and agents working for the Office for the Protection of the Constitution.

As early as 1998, he had criticized serious failings during the implementation of a search warrant against the neo-Nazi trio. From then on, the area would no longer be his concern.

Melzer says he did not join the demonstrations in 1989 in order to keep his mouth shut.

---

(2) Eike Sanders, social scientist, Berlin

COMMITMENT TO COMBATING NAZIS

Berlin social scientist Eike Sanders's work for the NSU Watch project involves making knowledge assembled for decades by anti-fascist projects available to the general public, while also organizing independent coverage of trials.

'I work for the Anti-Fascist Education and Press Center in Berlin, and I have now started with NSU Watch in the independent monitor Inform & Intervene, covering the NSU trial in Munich. Our reason for setting up the blog was that we feel there is a growing need for independent research, and for an independent evaluation of incoming intelligence.'

NSU Watch attempts to pool knowledge and information that has been collected in anti-fascist projects for decades, and to employ expertise in making it available to the public. Eike Sanders herself also attends the sessions of the German Bundestag's Committee of Inquiry.

'I find the work done by parliamentarians there impressive; at the same time, it is clear that what we are dealing with here is merely a fraction of the overall picture. What is especially important here is exposing the so-called failure of the authorities.'

NSU Watch and the Berlin association apabiz (Antifascist Press Archive and Education Center) are concerned first and foremost with revealing the bigger picture of a neo-Nazi scene that provided the ideological and logistic background for terrorist activity, a network that allowed the murderers to live and mount their attacks undetected. What they want to find out is 'what these people actually did, what they think, what kind of ideologies can be identified in the neo-Nazi scene, how they prepared for armed struggle. Sure, the authorities have gathered their own intelligence on this, but it was well-known even back in the 90s that independent research was also up and running and was fully necessary, that society needed to know what was going on, and that intel on neo-Nazis existed that the authorities did not have. Perhaps they didn't have it because they didn't want it, or perhaps because, as always, they underestimated the level of danger even then.'

Many at NSU Watch and apabiz work on a voluntary basis. Apabiz receives support from the Berlin Senate as part of its program against rightwing extremism and also runs a blog especially for Berlin: Berlin Outside Right.

'Apabiz is a registered charity; it is an anti-fascist press archive and education centre based in Berlin. At its heart is a large archive where for some time—it was our 20th anniversary two years ago, and the holdings go back as far as the 1950s—we have collected stuff that the neo-Nazi scene or extreme right have, in the widest sense, published themselves. We also do educational work and publish our own material on the subject.'

The state authorities do not seem to have accessed this material; it is possible they do read the blog, however. Apabiz has never been approached directly. Eike Sanders, a Social Sciences graduate, began working here on a voluntary basis and was eventually employed by the association some six and a half years ago. 'A lot of heart's blood' has gone into this work, she says, dedicated political motivation and personal commitment to thwarting the Nazis. On the trial against Zschäpe and others, she says: 'You just have to look at the number of witnesses summoned. I think there are more than 600 named, many of them certainly officials of various kinds, but also people from the scene, although who knows how much they'll be prepared to say.'

In spite of the considerable scope of the trial, Eike Sanders is aware of the limits set by criminal proceedings to anything like a full clarification of the NSU complex.

'Of the initiatives that contributed to setting up NSU Watch, apabiz is only one of a dozen. It is also worth mentioning a.i.d.a. in Munich. And everyone involved is networked. We are in touch with accessory prosecution lawyers as well as with the families of victims of the Keupstraße bomb attack and series of racist murders.'

By setting up NSU Watch, the movement has created its own transregional structure, thereby relieving pressure on other projects that have a local focus. The work demands a great deal from all involved: Eike Sanders knows how important it is to approach this subject in a realistic, level-headed manner, while not forgetting her own security. Sometimes neo-Nazis turn up in her dreams. But she also has friends who have nothing to do with her work, and she enjoys dancing and sport.

———————

(3) Thomas Grund, outreach social-worker, Jena

COMPANY THE NSU-PERPETRATORS KEPT

Outreach social worker Thomas Grund works at the 'Hugo' youth centre in Jena. Beate Zschäpe and Uwe Mundlos often visited the club before their time as NSU-terrorists.

'After the end of the GDR there was a group of older skins in Jena. They had become skins, far-right skins, in the mid-1980s, and, as early as 89, 90, 91, had started raiding any place in Jena they didn't like the look of.'

Thomas Grund has worked at the 'Hugo' youth club in Jena-Winzerla since 1991, before which he worked for the Lutheran Church. Before that he was a glass-blower. He started youth work, with the kids 'out there', as he puts it, because he hates being tied to a desk. He likes to be active, organizing concerts and competitions for bands. He filmed Beate Zschäpe and others in Winzerla, sitting on some steps outside, a bottle of beer in her hand.

'When I think of Beate—she had turned up with a group in the summer of 91, and I did this interview with her, in June I think it was—it all happened by chance. There she was, sitting on a bench with the two or three people I was interviewing about their everyday life in the area. I knew them, but hardly knew Beate at all, only this group and the scene they were in, and maybe her grandmother or whoever it was who looked after her, and I must say, to me she seemed like a country bumpkin.'

Grund—nickname: Cactus—sets up a club team, a party room, games, trips—including to Auschwitz—a bar run by members. Beate Zschäpe is in the club team. Uwe Mundlos is there too, his hair always correctly parted, German-style, wearing jump boots and a bomber jacket. Eventually they and a couple of other youths break into the club and steal cash and equipment. The social workers withdraw the complaint they've filed, but insist on victim-offender mediation. When they go round to Mundlos's home, they see a German Reich War Ensign displayed in the kids' room.

Ralph Wohlleben, a co-defendant in the Zschäpe trial, accused of aiding and abetting, gets one of his cronies to hire the party room and, as his birthday invitation, distributes leaflets with the logo 'No entry for immigrants' accompanied by the usual far-right symbols.

They call Thomas Grund a 'lefty louse'. Week for week, right-wingers gather in front of the clubhouse forming two lines through which the youths are forced to pass on their way into the concerts. Grund accompanies participants to see them safely home. By this time, Grund is no longer letting right-wingers into the clubhouse. After a while, the terror stopped.

'I thought they must have left the country because they weren't making any inroads here. Perhaps they'd gone via Holland to Sweden, where the far-right scene has a completely different standing and is able to develop a more open public profile than in Germany, and where they would be able to go underground for a while. I was utterly convinced that was the case, until Day X, when it became obvious they hadn't gone underground at all.'

When it turned out on 11 November 2011 that the terrorist trio had committed murders and robbed banks, Thomas Grund organized a meeting for former participants and members. People who had been between 18 and 20 when the Wall came down discussed their experiences of the period. For a while they had been fellow travellers of at least two of the later perpetrators. It was the 90s: 'Suddenly anything was possible. You could study if you wanted, you could travel, buy this or that, even move away and live elsewhere... So what happened to them? How come they didn't get their act together?' asks one participant in the discussion.

The discussions are available on YouTube under the heading 'Krachi'. Another group of youths takes a video camera to see Böhnhardt's parents. The interviewer ends up weeping. At home he was always a nice boy, say the parents.

'When the news came through that they had stayed in Germany the whole time since disappearing in '98, it was obvious they couldn't have done that without help from some very important people. It just wouldn't have been possible. There must have been people high up, people in positions of authority who would have been able cover up various things so nobody saw what was going on.'

Thomas Grund sees social work as a way of helping young people organize their own lives, as support for when they make mistakes. Where is it important to draw a line? Above the entrance of Jena's Lutheran Young Community centre is the sentence: 'They came from here'.

■■■■■■■■

(4) Kutlu Yurtseven, musician, Cologne

VICTIMS OF NSU PLACED UNDER SUSPICION

The residents of Keupstraße were subject to unfair investigations for years, Kutlu Yurtseven complains.

At the time of the 2004 Cologne nail-bomb attack, Kutlu Yurtseven was himself a Keupstraße resident. He lived there for eight years: 'Keupstraße is a kind of Mecca for Turkish confectioneries, pastries, food in general. There's always something going on down on the street.'

That day, Kutlu Yurtseven was stopped. He saw the first casualties, including a friend he played football with.

'Of course, you ask yourself what's going on in the shops, what's with your friends. That was four or five hours after the attack. You could feel the panic. There was a truck: it's known the brunt of the blast and nails was taken by this small truck, otherwise somebody would've definitely been killed.'

Keupstraße had always been an area that attracted immigrants and foreigners. After the attack, the percentage of Germans who came to the area was pretty well zero. The business community not only had to live with their own anxiety but also made considerable financial losses in the years that followed. As far as the human dimension of things was concerned, the scandal, as Kutlu Yurtseven calls it, was 'that we were the ones who were immediately blamed and pilloried, and the story was that it was all some internal Turkish feud between the Turkish Hezbollah, the PKK and the protection mafia, or tradesmen who couldn't see eye to eye. The police investigation just wasn't fair.'

Merely having something to do with Keupstraße, or with friends and business partners there, was enough to arouse suspicion. Kutlu Yurtseven tells the story of a lady whose husband was active politically and immediately found herself treated as a suspect. Within one and a half hours of the attack, the special police force SEK paid her and her child a visit, an enounter from which they have not recovered to this day. According to Yurtseven, they are traumatized. They are still afraid of the police.

Working with friends he put together a program of films. The special thing about the so-called Keupstraße Cinema, which lasted until the beginning of April 2013, was that the films were shown in shops, cafés and restaurants. With the support of the chairperson of the local Keupstraße community group, Mitat Bey, they were able to gain the citizens' trust and eventually more and more people came. After the showings, they talked about the films, also about themselves and their own experiences.

The cinema helped bring various facts to light, because people would come along and pluck up the courage to start talking. They talked of what they had witnessed, about the experience of being a victim of the attack, and about what they suffered under the police investigations that followed. Kutlu Yurtseven wants to show just how perfidious police procedure was and how important it is to talk about these things, so they don't happen again.

The residents' situation was totally desperate, he says: 'Many are frightened because they don't know where to turn with their complaints. Are we supposed to complain to the police about the police? It's impossible. The thing is we were let down by the authorities, by our fellow human beings too. That's why we need to go to the people themselves and ask for their own experiences.'

For Kutlu Yurtseven, it is important 'to tell this story from the perspective of the victims and not, as usual, from on high. In the meantime, they are not merely victims, which is unfortunately inescapable anyway, but some are also plaintiffs and complainants, and are saying: look, this is what was done to us, you kept silent about it and let us suffer for some eight years, although you eventually knew yourselves what the truth was, and that is what this is about.'

Many of the Keupstraße residents have found lawyers and become joint plaintiffs in the NSU trial. Kutlu Yurtseven and his friends still organize discussions—they are thinking about making a documentary film that bears witness to the events in the Keupstraße and shows the continued suspicions held by the investigative authorities towards the victims themselves, as well as the fact that traumatized residents have received no offer of help—not even an apology.

<hr/>

(5) Katharina König, politician, Jena

DISMAY OVER THE INTELLIGENCE AGENCIES

For some time, the authorities in her home town of Jena have made a bogeyman of the Left while ignoring far-right extremism, says Katharina König, a member of the State Parliament of Thuringia.

Katharina König is a politician. Her struggle with the neo-Nazi scene in Jena, where she was born and grew up, began in the 1990s. In the Thuringian Committee of Inquiry, she plays an important role in throwing light on how the three terrorists Mundlos, Böhnhardt and Zschäpe escaped arrest and kept such a low profile.

'I was beaten up by neo-Nazis for the first time at the beginning of 1993 when I was 14 or almost 15, and it was immediately obvious to me that there was no way around it: this was something that had to be dealt with. If only for one's own protection, at least to start with.'

This led her to the Left, who were in the process of forming a group to collect information, organize meetings in the community and gather moral courage.

'It's so you are not alone in the world when something like that happens, and that's why JG Stadtmitte became the first port of call for us all in the 1990s.'

JG Stadtmitte is the Young Community of the Lutheran Church, of which Katharina's father, Lothar König, is pastor. From 1995/96 onward, she belonged to an activist community of varied outlook whose members collected information and paid attention whenever the far right organized concerts or bought houses, monitoring their organizing tactics and the details of their attacks.

After leaving school, she spent more than a year in Israel before studying Semitic Studies and attaining a final qualification in Arabic. She decided to become a social worker and worked for seven years as a social education worker and in community youth work, before entering the Thuringian State Parliament in 2009 for the left-wing party, Die Linke.

Katharina König enjoys the support of her family. Her parents were involved in organizing counter-demonstrations, in which they encouraged people to take part with their children.

'The terrible thing is that the neo-Nazis beat up kids just because of their appearance. They attack anything and anyone that right-wingers see as alternative. To begin with it was the punks. Then came the immigrants, although even today there are not many immigrants in Jena. But any immigrants that there are have, I think, had to deal with neo-Nazis. And then, just as mad, anybody who was not a Nazi and just trying to get on as a normal kid, they would target them too.'

For years this kind of thing went on without attracting much attention.

'The standard procedures and conduct of the police betrayed their neglect. They didn't really investigate, or not so that those under threat or who were actually attacked noticed the effect. Complaints to the police rarely led to convictions of neo-Nazis. Local government, the mayor and the town council, claimed prosecutions would just lead to the creation of enemy stereotypes, and that Jena was no worse than other cities.'

The authorities had tended to see their enemy on the left, while hundreds of criminal offences by right-wingers went unpunished. What has come to light in the meantime shows that the vilified, discredited and even criminalized anti-fascist groups were right all along. At the same time, Katharina König doubts 'that the committees of inquiry will ever be able to uncover the truth, or if so, there will be different truths.'

The kind of truth the victims' families have been waiting for will never be found, neither by the committees of inquiry nor by the trial against Zschäpe and others, says König.

Nonetheless, week for week, she continues reading the 2 million unredacted pages passed on for the Committee's scrutiny. And every day new information arrives: to date some two truck-loads.

She is horrified by the spying activities of the Office for the Protection of the Constitution, the way they pay unofficial informants and hush up the criminal activities of undercover collaborators. An organization like that has no place in a democracy, she says.

'MY TEXT MUST HOLD TRUE IN THE EYES OF THOSE
WHO HAVE SUFFERED'

ESTHER DISCHEREIT IN CONVERSATION WITH INSA WILKE

On 2 September 2013, the Bundestag debated the final report of the NSU Committee of Inquiry. At about the same time, a number of radio stations broadcast Esther Dischereit's Klagelieder (Lamentations), *dedicated to the families of the NSU victims, in Turkish and German. Prior to the broadcast, literary critic Insa Wilke spoke to Esther Dischereit about the project.*

INSA WILKE. It is often said that writing should be more 'up-to-date'. You are currently working with material that could hardly be more top-ical: the NSU murders. How come?

ESTHER DISCHEREIT. In November 2011, giving a reading to the Jewish Community in Venice, I heard about the NSU murders. The audi-ence was disturbed by the news that right-wing extremists had been committing murders for years in Germany with impunity: nobody had put a stop to their activities. At the time, I think my audience had already understood the full magnitude of the crimes better than I had. Not long afterwards, I was approached by a composer for a libretto, and it was immediately clear to me that I wanted to research and write about the NSU. I need to write about things that seriously bother me.

WILKE. The German newspaper DIE ZEIT used the headline: 'Beate, the brown widow' (brown being a colour associated with Nazism). There was considerable interest in romantic aspects of the three-way relationship between these supposed 'natural-born killers'. How do you plan to avoid that kind of tackiness?

DISCHEREIT. The killers dominated the media; I wanted to focus on the victims and those affected by their deaths. But how? I wasn't up for a requiem with sublime language; I wanted to write about the victims' everyday lives, and the loss felt by their families even today whenever they think of some particular characteristic of their loved ones, or of something he or she used to do. Or sometimes memories become attached to objects. How had these people been earning their living for the previous decades? Here, too, the reports were one-sided, often portraying the victims as poor people from foreign countries. A doctor from an immigrant background wasn't murdered. The 'florist' Enver Şimşek was actually a wholesaler. You could call him a successful businessman, but he has ended up a 'florist'. Their choice of victims suggests the perpetrators planned to annihilate those to whom the attributes 'poor and foreign' or 'impoverished' would translate into 'underclass'. The language of the authorities did nothing to reverse this stigmatization. Ranking people according to their educational 'class' has always been a problem in Germany. As far as showing these things on the stage was concerned, I needed to find a way to get beyond this notion of 'otherness', away from foreign labelling and pauperization. I needed to go back to Othello, or 'Otello' as I call him. I had thought a lot about him a few years earlier when I was involved in a translation project about the way Shakespeare deals with Blackness.

WILKE. And where exactly do you see the link to the NSU case?

DISCHEREIT. The series of murders by the NSU was racially motivated, but I could also see how they constituted an attempt to demote the entire group—anybody from a Turkish ethnic background—to a lower social level, as if they belonged to a lower stage of human development. As a matter of fact, the victims of far-right violence in the past had often been homeless people. As militant aggression, then, it had an ambiguous nature: an ethnic and a social aspect, simultaneously. Ideologically speaking, such acts are based on the neo-Nazi notion of 'worthless life'. But how, in my writing, was I going to approach the owner of a grocery, or someone who ran a locksmith service, or a Siemens shift worker? During their lifetime, their social status would not have made them visible in any public sense. Their everyday working life was unremarkable—which was something else the investigating authorities saw differently. These people slogged away, their lengthy working hours probably typical of small to middling self-employed firms, that sort of thing. There was no resemblance to the kind of material through which Émile Zola denounced horrific working conditions, nor to the subject matter of West Side Story for that matter, where a poor girl from a poor family might try her luck. I was obsessed with the notion that the solution to the problem lay with 'Otello'. Otello was a shining light. So I brought him together with characters who, on stage, represent the murdered people. He was an acclaimed general; he had won fame and honour and had climbed to the very 'top'. But his ruin came through the kind of racism the other people, the ones we are talking about now, also suffered.

WILKE. But surely Othello's downfall was the result of envy and the machinations of those who resented his success.

DISCHEREIT. In Othello's case, racism achieves its effect by inversion. He is exposed to naked discrimination and denunciation, and at first seems capable of overcoming the problem, but he is ultimately unable to shake off the racist reservations of his milieu, the increasing aggressions directed against him. His inability to deconstruct the situation ultimately leads to his conforming to hostile imputations; he absorbs them into his body and is poisoned by them. He starts to think of himself in terms that others have attributed to him: Do you really believe that Desdemona, a beautiful white woman, wants a 'Moor'? In fact, there is not the slightest reason for him to doubt his wife's faithfulness. But someone who is constantly vilified by others will eventually see himself as vile. It is doubting his equality with Desdemona's equals that makes him commit the terrible deed.

WILKE. Are you saying that in the case of the NSU there is this second crime that followed the murders?

DISCHEREIT. It was a follow-up crime whose scope was not clear to me when I was actually writing. I only grasped these things gradually because I didn't know enough about the detail of how these investigations were carried out. And sometimes I simply ran away from the facts.

Those who suffered most from this kind of racist inversion were the widows who were shown pictures by the investigating officers of blonde women with whom their husbands were allegedly having affairs. This was a total fabrication that broke the widows' hearts and undermined whole families. The investigators have gone unpunished to this day.

WILKE. You have said that it was difficult to maintain a balance between pathos, prayer and the quotidian in your writing. I see a different problem: it was said of the politically committed writers of the 1970s that they claimed to be giving minorities and socially disadvantaged groups a voice, but did not actually let them speak. By not doing so, it was said they were as guilty as everybody else of ignoring, patronizing and discrimination

DISCHEREIT. The idea to begin with was that the libretto would also be a platform for anybody who wanted to speak out. I informed one of the families' lawyers of this and spoke about it on the radio as well. It was only later that I actually met any of the families. Events overtook my proposal. The voices of affected families were eventually heard, in TV features and other media. Semiya Şimşek published her book *Schmerzliche Heimat* (Painful Homeland). The question I was now asking was a different one: when others use the victims' story for their own ends, does it not make an exhibition of their suffering, like displaying it in a shop window? There is also the danger of re-traumatizing the victims and adding to their pain. Some want to speak or want their story to be told, others don't. So the question now became: how do I speak not about them, but from alongside them, at their side. During this process, people who were intent on finding out the truth about the crimes encouraged me in my thinking. They communicated to me that my work was giving emotional support to the affected families. Under the aegis of Kenan Kolat,

President of the Turkish Community in Germany at the time, and his team, we came together and listened to a production of the *Klagelieder* (*Lamentations*), which form a part of the opera and which were broadcast by Deutschlandradio Kultur. Everybody was very encouraging.

WILKE. Your intention is not only to give a voice to those affected. You have also said you want to give expression to public mourning.

DISCHEREIT. The investigators investigated and are still searching for the truth, the journalists write their reports; I am an author. In my writing I wanted to 'accommodate' others, not speak on their behalf, which is something else again. The meaning of mourning in the public sphere has always played a strong role in my work. It's 'we' who are responsible for having been incapable of protecting the citizens who used to be my neighbours. Whenever I think of this, I find myself remembering the Greek tragic character Antigone. Mourning is a particularly archaic way of enabling a society to reflect on itself and its values. The real question is, then, whether 'we' are in a position to mourn. I think we have to.

In order to mourn, there first has to be an understanding of what has happened.

The German government's memorial event following the exposure of the NSU pointed the way, although they have not kept their promise of total clarification, nor have they put much effort into doing so. We'll have to see how things progress. A lot still has to be done before we feel the truth has been uncovered. Beyond the official political scene, who is actually there to support those who have suffered this loss? In Munich, I met the owner of a jazz bar, a Herr Vogler, who collected money to give to the families of the victims. I had the feeling this was pretty exceptional. The big influential organizations, the trade unions and the churches, where are they? The defamation of the victims and their milieu has evidently been so successful that the investigation is moving too slowly and people are denying empathy. The Turkish communities are saying: who is there for us—the Jews, the Sinti and Roma, the lesbians and gays. Where is everybody else?

WILKE. Would the reaction have been different if the crimes had been perpetrated by left-wing extremists?

DISCHEREIT. The question did occasionally arise during Committee of Inquiry sessions. Would the authorities have reacted differently if a top banker had been murdered? They probably would. When RAF member Wolfgang Grams was shot, the Minister of the Interior resigned. At the time, there was evidently a different understanding of what constituted a breach of the political consensus. However, there are no real grounds for comparison because the Offices for Protection of the Constitution have the entire spectrum of the extreme left—often including associations like the Anti-fascist Archive and the educational centre a.i.d.a. in Munich—under constant observation, along with the Islamist terror scene. At the same time, departments that were supposed to focus on right-wing extremism were dismantled or in some places didn't exist in the first place.

WILKE. In January 2013, you said you still found it difficult to understand why 13 years had passed after the NSU had gone underground without the authorities taking any action at all, a period in which they utterly failed to do their job, as the final report of the Bundestag's Committee of Inquiry describes. Have you gained a different perspective following your many years of working on the case as a writer?

DISCHEREIT. It is clear that racist and ethnocentric clichés have underpinned the kinds of investigative praxis we have seen to date. That is hardly surprising in a society in which the vast majority of the population is white and which has little sense of itself as country of immigration. The conduct of the authorities was devastating and has meant a second wave of trauma for the families. The onus of proof in cases of racism still rests with the affected parties rather than the other way around. There are shadowy areas too that continue to elude investigation. This is particularly true in the case of the deployment of undercover agents, which has defied all scrutiny or control, and has led to a massive, state-sanctioned arming and strengthening of far-right extremism. It is now at least possible to reconstruct, in almost minute detail, the unfolding of events during the legendary police failure to make arrests in Thüringen, but the question nonetheless remains as to whether this occurred 'for certain reasons', or whether it was, as we generally prefer to see it, the result of unparalleled incompetence. These questions remain unanswered, as do the questions of how many murderers and accomplices there really were, or how the two we do know about died.

WILKE. Do you think it was right to terminate the work of the German Bundestag's Committee of Inquiry?

DISCHEREIT. Closing down the Committee meant ending its search for—and discovery of—the real facts. The accessory prosecution lawyers published a press statement setting this out and explaining why the actions of the Minister of the Interior had been counter-productive. Where in the world can a Ministry of the Interior remove and shred files with impunity at the very moment when those files are required for a parliamentary control committee? It has to be asked whether what we are looking at here is a criminal offence. Or in a different matter: what are we looking at when on-duty police officers lie to citizens? Giving someone to understand that a matter has been uncovered in a police investigation when in fact it is entirely fabricated, for example: your husband was having an affair—isn't that a form of subversion? And is subversion of this kind a permissible tool of criminal investigation? Hardly. The public think the investigating authorities have a responsibility to speak the truth. A truck driver who causes grievous damage in his line of work, and be it through negligence or condoning acceptance of a crime, is answerable for his actions. However, the Minister for the Interior did not feel responsible in any way. That is peculiar, and I find such matters distressing.

WILKE. The NSU came out of the far-right milieu of the 1990s. In your libretto, you repeatedly refer to the importance of German Unification for these crimes. How would you characterize the milieu, given that it formed after Unification?

DISCHEREIT. The social and political upheavals after 1989 gave rise to an anti-democratic milieu. This became the humus for a particularly virulent coalition of right-wing extremists from East and West. They received support for this project, too, by which I mean the practice of financing them via undercover contacts, for example, despite it's being already clear to what extent these people were ready to use violence. It is hard to grasp why far-right extremists were not punished without further ado. I have spoken to police officers who simply cannot understand why the pogroms in Rostock-Lichtenhagen were allowed to happen, why the various security agencies did not intervene. And that was not the only success the Right had, because asylum law was made more restrictive too. Their violence had been answered with a political retreat. Populists and the militant far right had entered a political alliance. The consequence was an erosion of democracy.

WILKE. 'What is wrong with us all?' asked Tülin Özüdoğru, the daughter of the second murder victim. Has writing given you an answer to her question?

DISCHEREIT. My question is not, 'What's wrong with us?' My question is: Can I really understand what is going on? As a motive for its most violent criminal form, namely murder, racism had taken on a scale I had not previously considered possible in the everyday reality of the Federal Republic. To be more exact, I had not foreseen the systematic nature of the killing, the conscious planning of murders and attacks. We had—and here I really am using the 'we' form—a consensus across society to concern ourselves with the consequences of National Socialism and the Holocaust. Persecution for 'racial' reasons and death threats against minorities were outlawed, tabooed and punished after 1945, although the vigour of the courts in bringing perpetrators to justice has left much to be desired. However, this series of murders has put the same kind of virulent threat to people's lives back on today's agenda. A minority is being targeted as a collective entity. It will take a lot to get the majority to understand that an exclusion of this nature is tantamount to dismantling the Republic. If people cannot live safely here, and I specifically include those who have fled dreadful civil wars and are now seeking protection in, for instance, Berlin-Hellersdorf, if these people are facing threats of danger to life and limb in the very place where they had hoped to find asylum, then something is morally rotten. Public discourse in this country had not envisaged the existence of a German Ku Klux Klan, nor was it capable of imagining that the officer-in-charge when policewoman Michèle Kiesewetter was murdered was a member of that organization. The Ku Klux Klan is no weekend playground for under-challenged boys.

WILKE. You bring an enlightenment approach to the work of the artist: you write in order to understand.

DISCHEREIT. Primarily it is myself I am trying to enlighten. There is a world of difference between a mediated report—something, let's say, communicated in the past tense—and the process of understanding itself. Somewhere between these poles, I have to suppress my urge to maintain a distance from these atrocities, not to allow myself to be personally affected. In fact, I am affected anyway, as a Jew, and as a citizen too, of course. What I have understood is that victim protection programs have to be improved, preferably by creating an independent institution, a kind of civic institute, where those affected by right-wing violence can get support. For instance, as we have seen here, victims of police violence can hardly be expected to turn to the same police if they wish to make a complaint. Laws need to be changed so that if someone from a migrant background comes to harm through criminal actions, the possibility of a racist motive is automatically taken into account. And I have also now understood how dangerous our secret services actually are. How could we tolerate a situation where they were involved in setting up violent right-wing terrorist groups via undercover agents? How could they know about these things and do nothing about them? It was important to ask myself too: What are we going to do with these people, of which there are several thousand? What does it feel like to be in contact with them, and is there any way at all in which they can be useful in future? The libretto offers a possible solution to this problem.

WILKE. Was the composer happy with your idea for the libretto?

DISCHEREIT. He was happy for me to do what I wanted. Later, however, he stepped back from the project, for personal reasons. I had really wanted to show the *Lamentations* to DJ İpek İpekçioğlu, whom I rated highly. I couldn't have said why; we had rarely seen each other, and only from a distance. She has Turkish roots, so that may have been one reason. Then the phone rang. And she did the soundtracks for the radio production of the *Lamentations*. That changed my way of thinking about possible ways of using music.

WILKE. Did you think about musical realization while writing?

DISCHEREIT. I always hear something when I write. Voices mainly. The most important thing—as I saw it—was to address what desperately needed to be said or described. Bits of subject matter, memories, file labels, shreds of detail that I thought had to be in there, because they allowed glimpses of the links and ramifications that had made this crime possible in all its monstrosity. In the course of this work, I have entered spaces that have not been fully investigated to this day. I have also included very different forms of expression: some scenes seem realistic, others surreal; semi-documentary material; also language types that resemble conceptual interventions; and there are poetic texts too. Other textual material collected here is meant for potential directors. When Otello appears, the tone changes. We listen across the centuries. I realize that very few texts are suited to musical settings for voice. I was quite uncompromising in this respect. But tonal contributions and soundscapes can be achieved by other means. The important thing is that the text holds true in the eyes of those who have suffered.

WILKE. In 2012, Milo Rau attempted to stage the recent case of a mass murder perpetrated by a right-wing extremist: Breivik's Statement. People felt it was a provocation and it was largely rejected because there was no appetite for right-wing propaganda on the stage. What have been your experiences with provocation?

DISCHEREIT. What interests me is how close up I can get to a process that, to begin with anyway, defied all comprehension. Like holding a magnifying glass up so closely it gets nasty. Of course, that can be felt as a provocation. But if so, that is just a secondary effect. I want to be quite unambiguous in my approach to this subject. I have no desire to reconstruct the feelings of the perpetrators. That's not my thing—not the side I'm on. Others can devote themselves to that if they feel like it.

WILKE. For you, diversity of voices was important here. There is no main character in your text. Why not?

DISCHEREIT. I didn't want to construct a 'plot'. I was disturbed by the way the victims were seen as a group, which, in reality, they never were. They were different people, individuals, separate biographies. This contradiction had concerned me when thinking about the dead and murdered of the Holocaust. In the libretto, I pursue this imposed group formation by looking at archives and lists and showing how people and their fates are filed away, reduced to catchwords and kept in boxes. That's one side of it. At the same time, I have created a series of separate scenes with individual characters like A.T. and E.

WILKE. What other routes of access to the subject do you have as an artist that would not be open to journalists, lawyers or politicians?

DISCHEREIT. The third level plays with the atmospheric background. I allege no linearity whatsoever, no direct connectedness to succeeding scenes. One example is the short sequence about the Jews in the eighteenth and nineteenth centuries. The forms of discrimination in that period show parallels to the legal and social status of the immigrant minorities of the present. I use a similar technique for the disappearance of the files. I depict the events as tangibly as possible, in a way that seems likely to me. And it isn't even invented. In some respects, art, and only art, allows me the freedom to express what we think. I can reverse the burden of proof.